Quality Assurance Testing from Beginner to Paid Professional

Part 1

Everything You Need to Know to Start a
Career in Manual and Automated QA Testing

Written By
Bolakale Aremu

Quality Assurance Testing from Beginner to Paid Professional, Part 1:
Everything You Need to Know to Start a Career in Manual and Automated QA Testing

ISBN: 979-8-3492-2790-5

Published in the United States

Limit of Liability/Disclaimer of Warranty

Table of Contents

Part 1: Introduction to Software Testing 7

1. Overview of Quality Assurance 7

1.1. What is Software Testing? 8

1.2. Importance of Quality Assurance in Software Development 10

1.2.1. Why Quality Assurance Matters 10

1.2.2. The Role of QA in the Software Development Lifecycle (SDLC) .. 11

1.3. Manual vs. Automated Testing – When to Use Each 12

1.3.1. What is Manual Testing? 12

1.3.2. What is Automated Testing? 13

1.3.3. Choosing the Right Approach 14

1.4. Skills Required to Become a QA Tester 15

Part 2: Fundamentals of Manual QA Testing 16

2: Understanding Quality Assurance 16

2.1. Definition of Quality Assurance (QA) 16

2.2. Key Aspects of QA 16

2.3. QA vs. Software Testing: Are They the Same? 16

2.4. Why is QA Important? 17

2.5. Role of QA in Software Development Lifecycle 18

2.6. QA in Different Phases of the SDLC 18

2.7. Benefits of QA in the SDLC 20

3. Foundations of Test Cases 21

3.1. Types of Software Testing (Functional vs. Non-Functional) 21

3.2. Test Case Design Principles 23

3.3. Writing Clear and Effective Test Cases 25

4. Designing Effective Test Cases 28

4.1. Positive and Negative Test Scenarios 28

4.2. Boundary Value Analysis and Equivalence Partitioning 30

4.3. Common Mistakes in Test Case Design 33

4.4. Organizing Test Cases for Maximum Efficiency 35

5. Test Case Management 40

5.1. Using Test Case Management Tools (Jira, TestRail, etc.) 40

5.2. Organizing Test Cases for Maximum Efficiency 43

5.3. Creating and Managing Test Suites 47

6. Test Execution and Bug Reporting 52

6.1. How to Execute Manual Test Cases 52

6.2. Identifying and Logging Bugs Properly 56

6.3. Writing Effective Bug Reports (Steps to Reproduce, Screenshots, etc.) 62

6.4. Common Bug Tracking Tools (Jira, Bugzilla, etc.) 68

Part 3: Transitioning from Manual to Automated Testing 75

7. Introduction to Automation in QA 75

7.1. What is Test Automation? 75

7.2. Benefits and Challenges of Automation 77

7.3. When to Automate and When Not To 79

8. Writing Automation Scripts 83

8.1. Basics of Programming for Testers (Python, Java, JavaScript) 83

8.2. Writing Your First Automation Script 87

8.3. Debugging and Troubleshooting Automation Scripts 94

8.4. Practice Exercises on writing, debugging, and optimizing automation scripts 100

Exercise 1: Automating a Simple Google Search 100

Exercise 2: Verifying a Login Functionality 100

Exercise 3: Handling a Dynamic Drop-Down Menu 101

Exercise 4: Scraping Multiple Elements from a Web Page 101

Exercise 5: Automating an End-to-End E-Commerce Checkout 102

8.5. Solutions to Practice Exercises 102

9. How to Get Your First QA Job 110

9.1. Writing a Strong QA Resume 110

9.2. Preparing for QA Interviews (Common Interview Questions) 112

9.3. Freelancing & Remote Work Opportunities in QA 116

9.4. Unlocking Part 2: Advanced QA Automation—Mastering Test Frameworks, API Testing, and CI/CD Integration 119

9.4.1. What You'll Learn in Part 2 of the Book 120

9.4.2. Be on the Lookout for Part 2! 122
9.5. How to Get Further Help & Support 123
10. References 124

where software testing comes in.

Software testing is the process of evaluating a software application to ensure it meets the required specifications and functions correctly. As a software tester, your job is to identify bugs, defects, or any issues that could affect the user experience. By systematically testing software, you help developers create reliable, high-quality applications that work as expected.

You can think of software testing as a quality assurance process that validates whether an application performs correctly under different conditions. It involves executing a program to find defects before it reaches the hands of users. Without proper testing, software may contain errors that could lead to security vulnerabilities, performance failures, or usability issues.

To be an effective tester, you must adopt a systematic approach. This means:

1. Understanding Requirements: Before you start testing, you need to know what the software is supposed to do. This involves reviewing specifications, user stories, or any documentation that outlines expected behavior.

2. Planning and Designing Tests: Once you understand the requirements, you create test cases—structured scenarios that outline what to test, how to test it, and what the expected outcome should be.

3. Executing Tests: This is where you run the software and check if it behaves as expected. You may perform manual testing (where you interact with the application yourself) or automated testing (where scripts and tools help run tests more efficiently).

4. Identifying and Reporting Defects: If you find a bug, you document it and report it to the development team so they can fix it.

5. Re-Testing and Regression Testing: After bugs are fixed, you test again to ensure that previous issues have been resolved and that no new problems have been introduced.

By following this structured approach, you contribute to the software development lifecycle (SDLC) and help deliver a product that is functional, reliable, and user-friendly. Learn more about SDLC here: https://en.wikipedia.org/wiki/Systems_development_life_cycle. Whether you are testing a small mobile app or a large enterprise system, the goal remains the same—ensuring software quality and customer satisfaction.

Later, you'll explore the different types of software testing and how each plays a critical role in the development process.

1.2. Importance of Quality Assurance in Software Development

Software development is not just about writing code—it's about creating reliable, high-performing, and secure applications that meet user expectations. Quality Assurance (QA) plays a crucial role in achieving this goal. Without proper QA, software can be prone to bugs, security vulnerabilities, and performance issues that can lead to customer dissatisfaction, financial losses, and even legal consequences.

1.2.1. Why Quality Assurance Matters

1. Prevents Costly Errors
Fixing bugs in the later stages of development—or worse, after release—can be extremely expensive. QA helps identify issues early, reducing the cost and effort needed for fixes.

2. Ensures Software Reliability
Users expect software to function correctly under various conditions. QA ensures that applications perform consistently, minimizing crashes, errors, and unexpected behaviors.

3. Enhances Security
Cybersecurity threats are a major concern in today's digital world. QA includes security testing to identify vulnerabilities before hackers can exploit them, protecting sensitive user data.

Pros of Manual Testing:

- Requires no additional tools or setup
- Ideal for exploratory and usability testing
- Allows for quick adaptation to UI changes

Cons of Manual Testing:

- Time-consuming and repetitive
- Prone to human error
- Not scalable for large projects

1.3.2. What is Automated Testing?

Automated testing uses scripts and tools to execute test cases, compare actual outcomes with expected results, and generate reports. It is useful for repetitive and large-scale testing.

When to Use Automated Testing

Automation is most effective when dealing with repetitive, time-sensitive, or large-scale testing scenarios, such as:

1. **Regression Testing**: Ensures that recent code changes do not break existing functionality.
2. **Performance Testing**: Simulating thousands of users interacting with an application cannot be done manually.
3. **Load and Stress Testing**: Helps determine how software behaves under heavy usage.
4. **Repeated Test Scenarios**: Tests that need to be run frequently, such as login verification, can be automated to save time.
5. **Complex Scenarios with Large Data Sets**: Automating tests for applications that handle extensive data processing is more efficient than manual testing.

Pros of Automated Testing:

- Faster execution of test cases
- Increases accuracy and consistency
- Enables large-scale and repetitive testing

Cons of Automated Testing:

- Requires initial investment in tools and setup
- Cannot replace human intuition for exploratory or usability testing
- Scripts must be maintained as the application evolves

1.3.3. Choosing the Right Approach

The decision to use manual or automated testing depends on factors like project size, test frequency, and complexity. In most cases, a hybrid approach—where both manual and automated testing are used—is the most effective strategy.

Factor	Manual Testing	Automated Testing
Project Size	Small to medium-sized projects	Large-scale projects
Test Frequency	One-time or infrequent tests	Repetitive or frequent tests
Test Complexity	Simple test cases, UI/UX tests	Complex logic, performance tests
Budget & Resources	Low budget, no special tools	Requires automation tools and setup

By understanding the strengths and limitations of each method, you can apply the right testing approach to ensure software quality while optimizing time and resources.

1.4. Skills Required to Become a QA Tester

Becoming a Quality Assurance (QA) tester requires a combination of **technical skills, analytical thinking, and attention to detail**. Whether you're starting a career in software testing or looking to advance, mastering these skills will help you excel in the field.

1. Technical Skills

While QA testing does not always require coding knowledge, understanding certain technical aspects can enhance your efficiency.

- **Basic Programming Knowledge:** Familiarity with programming languages like Python, Java, or JavaScript can help in writing automated test scripts.
- **Understanding of Software Development Life Cycle (SDLC):** Knowing how software is developed helps in identifying where testing fits into the process.
- **Knowledge of Testing Tools:** Experience with testing tools such as **Selenium, JUnit, TestNG, Postman, JIRA, and Appium** is essential for both manual and automated testing.
- **Database and SQL Knowledge:** Many applications interact with databases, so understanding how to query data using SQL is beneficial.
- **Version Control Systems:** Familiarity with Git and GitHub helps in collaborating with developers and managing test scripts. Learn more about Git and GitHub here: https://www.youtube.com/watch?v=RGOj5yH7evk.

Part 2: Fundamentals of Manual QA Testing

2: Understanding Quality Assurance

2.1. Definition of Quality Assurance (QA)

Quality Assurance (QA) is a **systematic process** that ensures software meets defined quality standards before it is released to users. It involves preventing defects in software rather than just detecting and fixing them. QA is an essential part of software development that focuses on improving **processes, methodologies, and best practices** to deliver a reliable and high-performing product.

Alternatively, you can define Quality Assurance (QA) as a **proactive approach** that establishes and maintains a set of **standards and procedures** to ensure software quality throughout the development lifecycle. Unlike Quality Control (QC), which focuses on identifying defects **after** development, QA aims to prevent issues **before** they occur by optimizing processes and enforcing quality checks.

2.2. Key Aspects of QA

- **Process-Oriented:** Focuses on improving software development workflows rather than just testing the final product.
- **Prevention Over Detection:** Helps prevent defects by following best practices, guidelines, and industry standards.
- **Consistency & Reliability:** Ensures that the software is **consistent, meets user expectations, and performs reliably** across different environments.

2.3. QA vs. Software Testing: Are They the Same?

Although QA and software testing are related, they are **not the same**:

Aspect	Quality Assurance (QA)	Software Testing
Focus	Process improvement, defect prevention	Detecting defects in the software
Approach	Proactive (before development)	Reactive (during or after development)
Goal	Ensure development follows best practices	Identify bugs and defects
Methods Used	Documentation, reviews, audits, standards enforcement	Manual testing, automation testing, debugging

QA ensures that software testing is carried out effectively, but its scope extends beyond testing to include **process improvement, compliance, and continuous monitoring**.

2.4. Why is QA Important?

- **Enhances Software Reliability** – Ensures that the software is stable, functional, and performs well.
- **Reduces Development Costs** – Fixing bugs earlier in the development cycle is **cheaper** than fixing them post-release.
- **Boosts Customer Satisfaction** – Well-tested and high-quality software improves **user experience and trust**.
- **Compliance with Industry Standards** – Many industries, such as healthcare and finance, require software to meet strict quality regulations.

Key Takeaway

Quality Assurance is more than just testing—it is a **strategic approach** to improving software quality by **preventing defects** and optimizing development processes. By implementing QA best practices, companies can deliver **high-quality, reliable, and user-friendly** applications.

2.5. Role of QA in Software Development Lifecycle

Quality Assurance (QA) plays a **critical role** in the **Software Development Lifecycle (SDLC)** by ensuring that software is developed with high standards from the initial planning phase to final deployment and maintenance. It is **not just about testing**—QA integrates into every stage of development to improve efficiency, reliability, and user satisfaction.

2.6. QA in Different Phases of the SDLC

QA is embedded throughout the **six main phases** of the SDLC, ensuring that quality checks and improvements happen at every step:

1. Requirement Analysis (Planning Phase)

- QA ensures that requirements are clear, complete, and testable.
- Prevents misunderstandings that could lead to defects later in development.
- Reviews software specifications and business needs.

2. Design Phase

- Ensures that the software architecture follows best practices and design standards.
- Conducts **design reviews** to identify potential risks early.
- Validates UI/UX wireframes for usability and consistency.

3. Development Phase (Coding Phase)

- Works with developers to ensure **coding standards and best practices** are followed.
- Implements **Static Code Analysis** to detect potential vulnerabilities.
- Promotes **Test-Driven Development (TDD)** where developers write tests before writing code.

4. Testing Phase

- Executes **manual and automated tests** to identify functional and performance issues.
- Conducts **Regression Testing** to ensure new updates do not break existing functionality.
- Uses **Bug Tracking Systems (like JIRA, Bugzilla)** to report and manage defects.

5. Deployment Phase

- Performs **User Acceptance Testing (UAT)** to verify that the software meets business needs.
- Ensures that the deployment process is smooth and error-free.
- Verifies system stability in a **production-like environment** before final release.

6. Maintenance & Continuous Improvement

- Monitors software performance and user feedback after release.
- Conducts **Post-Release Testing** to catch any issues that arise in real-world use.
- Continuously improves the QA process based on past experiences and new industry standards.

2.7. Benefits of QA in the SDLC

- **Prevents Costly Errors** – Detecting issues early reduces development costs and avoids expensive post-release fixes.
- **Improves Software Reliability** – Ensures that software is stable, secure, and user-friendly before it reaches customers.
- **Enhances Collaboration** – Encourages teamwork between developers, testers, and business stakeholders for better results.
- **Customer Satisfaction** – Helps in delivering high-quality software that meets user expectations.

Key Takeaway

QA is not just a final step in software development—it is a **continuous process** that ensures quality from the very beginning of the SDLC. By integrating QA practices at every phase, organizations can develop software that is **robust, secure, and reliable** while reducing costs and risks.

3. Foundations of Test Cases

3.1. Types of Software Testing (Functional vs. Non-Functional)

Software testing is broadly classified into **Functional Testing** and **Non-Functional Testing**, each serving a unique purpose in ensuring software quality. While functional testing focuses on whether the software behaves as expected, non-functional testing assesses aspects like performance, security, and usability.

1. Functional Testing

Functional testing verifies that the software's features and functionalities work according to specified requirements. It focuses on the **"what"** of the system—ensuring that inputs produce the expected outputs.

Key Characteristics of Functional Testing:

- Ensures the system behaves as expected based on business and technical requirements.
- Involves **both manual and automated** testing methods.
- Uses **black-box testing** techniques, meaning testers do not need to understand the internal code structure.

Types of Functional Testing:

- **Unit Testing** – Testing individual components or functions in isolation.
- **Integration Testing** – Checking if different modules or services work together correctly.
- **System Testing** – Evaluating the entire system as a whole.
- **User Acceptance Testing (UAT)** – Performed by end users to validate whether the software meets business needs.
- **Regression Testing** – Ensuring that new updates do not introduce defects in existing functionality.

2. Non-Functional Testing

Non-functional testing focuses on how well the software performs under various conditions. It assesses software **quality attributes** like **speed, security, usability, and scalability** rather than functional correctness.

Key Characteristics of Non-Functional Testing:

- Evaluates system performance, security, and reliability.
- Helps identify bottlenecks that may impact the user experience.
- Often requires specialized tools for automation and load simulation.

Types of Non-Functional Testing:

- **Performance Testing** – Measures the software's speed, response time, and scalability.
- **Load Testing** – Determines how the system handles increased user traffic.
- **Stress Testing** – Tests system stability under extreme conditions.
- **Security Testing** – Identifies vulnerabilities that could be exploited by hackers.
- **Usability Testing** – Assesses how user-friendly the software is.
- **Compatibility Testing** – Ensures the software works across different devices, browsers, and operating systems.

Key Differences: Functional vs. Non-Functional Testing

Aspect	Functional Testing	Non-Functional Testing
Focus	What the software does	How the software performs
Goal	Ensures correct functionality	Evaluates quality attributes
Testing Approach	Uses black-box testing	Uses simulation tools & monitoring
Example	Checking login functionality	Measuring page load speed

Why Are Both Types Important?

- **Functional Testing** ensures that users get the features they expect.
- **Non-Functional Testing** ensures that users get a **fast, secure, and reliable experience**.
- Both types of testing **complement each other**, leading to a **well-rounded software product**.

Key Takeaway

Both functional and non-functional testing are essential for building software that is not only feature-rich but also fast, secure, and reliable. Functional testing ensures correctness, while non-functional testing enhances the overall user experience.

3.2. Test Case Design Principles

Designing effective test cases is crucial for ensuring software quality. Well-structured test cases help identify defects early, improve test coverage, and make testing more efficient. In this section, you'll explore the key principles that guide test case design.

1. Clarity and Simplicity

A good test case should be **clear, concise, and easy to understand**. Anyone reading it should know exactly what needs to be tested, how to test it, and what the expected outcome should be.

- **Use simple, precise language** to avoid confusion.
- **Avoid unnecessary complexity**—each test case should focus on a specific function or scenario.
- **Include step-by-step instructions** for execution.

2. Coverage and Completeness

Your test cases should cover all important features and scenarios of the software. Incomplete test cases can leave critical defects undetected.

- Ensure **both positive and negative test scenarios** are included.
- Focus on **high-risk and frequently used functionalities** first.
- Use **equivalence partitioning and boundary value analysis** to maximize coverage (discussed in Chapter 4).

3. Reusability

Well-designed test cases should be reusable across multiple testing cycles and projects.

- **Use modular test cases** that can be easily updated when needed.
- **Avoid redundant test cases**—if a scenario is already covered, don't duplicate it.
- **Leverage templates** to maintain consistency.

4. Maintainability and Scalability

Your test cases should be easy to maintain as the software evolves.

- **Use clear identifiers** (e.g., TC001, TC002) to track test cases.
- **Organize test cases** logically using test case management tools like Jira, TestRail, or Excel.
- **Update test cases** whenever new features are added or old features are modified.

5. Independent and Self-Contained

Each test case should be able to run independently, without relying on other test cases. This ensures that failures can be traced easily.

- Avoid dependencies on previous test cases.
- Each test case should have its own setup and teardown steps**,** if necessary.

6. Measurable and Testable Outcomes

Every test case should have a **clear expected result** that can be verified.

- Define expected outcomes in **specific, measurable terms** (e.g., "The login button should redirect to the dashboard").
- Use **assertions in automated testing** to compare actual vs. expected results.

Key Takeaway

By following these test case design principles, you can create structured, reliable, and effective test cases. This improves testing efficiency and ensures high-quality software.

In the next section, you'll learn **how to write clear and effective test cases** using these principles.

3.3. Writing Clear and Effective Test Cases

Writing well-structured test cases is essential for ensuring software quality. Clear and effective test cases help testers identify defects, ensure test coverage, and streamline the testing process. In this section, you'll learn the best practices for writing test cases that are easy to understand, execute, and maintain.

1. Use a Standardized Test Case Format

A well-defined test case structure improves readability and consistency. A typical test case includes:

- **Test Case ID** – A unique identifier (e.g., TC001, TC002).
- **Test Title** – A short, descriptive name (e.g., "Verify login with valid credentials").
- **Test Description** – A brief explanation of what the test covers.
- **Preconditions** – Any setup required before executing the test (e.g., "User must be registered").
- **Test Steps** – Step-by-step instructions to execute the test.
- **Expected Result** – The expected behavior of the system.
- **Actual Result** – The observed outcome after execution (recorded

during testing).
Status – Whether the test has **Passed, Failed**, or is **Blocked.**

2. Keep Test Cases Simple and Clear

Your test cases should be easy to read and understand.

- Use **simple, direct language** to describe steps and expected outcomes.
- Avoid technical jargon unless necessary.
- Write in an **active voice** (e.g., "Click the login button" instead of "The login button should be clicked").

3. Make Test Cases Self-Contained

Each test case should be independent and not rely on other test cases.

- **Avoid dependencies** – If one test case fails, it shouldn't cause others to fail.
- **Include preconditions** to set up the necessary test environment.

4. Cover Both Positive and Negative Scenarios

Testing should include both expected and unexpected user behaviors.

- **Positive test cases** verify that the software works as intended (e.g., entering valid login credentials).
- **Negative test cases** check how the system handles errors (e.g., entering an incorrect password multiple times).

5. Prioritize High-Risk and Critical Test Cases

Not all test cases have the same impact. Focus on:

- **Core functionalities** that impact users the most.
- **Edge cases** that are likely to break the system.
- **Security and performance-related scenarios.**

6. Use Realistic and Meaningful Test Data

- Use **valid test data** for positive scenarios (e.g., real email formats).
- Include **invalid inputs** for negative testing (e.g., special characters in a username field).
- Avoid using **hardcoded test data**—use data-driven testing where possible. "Hardcoded test data" refers to fixed or static values that are manually written into test cases, scripts, or the application itself, rather than being dynamically generated or fetched from an external source.

7. Make Test Cases Reusable

Test cases should be designed for future test cycles.

- **Use modular test steps** that can be reused in multiple scenarios.
- **Avoid redundancy** – If a test case already exists, don't duplicate it.

Key Takeaway

Writing clear and effective test cases ensures accurate testing, reduces ambiguity, and improves software reliability. By following these best practices, you can create high-quality test cases that enhance testing efficiency.

In the next chapter, you'll learn how to design effective test scenarios, including boundary value analysis and equivalence partitioning.

4. Designing Effective Test Cases

4.1. Positive and Negative Test Scenarios

In software testing, creating well-defined test scenarios is crucial for verifying that an application functions correctly and handles unexpected inputs gracefully. Test scenarios fall into two main categories: positive test scenarios and negative test scenarios.

1. What Are Positive and Negative Test Scenarios?

Positive Test Scenarios focus on testing the system's expected behavior using valid inputs. These tests confirm that the software functions correctly when used as intended.

Negative Test Scenarios assess how the system handles invalid, unexpected, or edge-case inputs. These tests help identify vulnerabilities, error-handling mechanisms, and potential crashes.

Both types of tests are essential for ensuring software quality and reliability.

2. Understanding Positive Test Scenarios

A **positive test scenario** ensures that the application behaves correctly when valid data is provided and correct user actions are performed.

Example: Testing a Login Page

- **Test Step:** Enter a valid username and password.
- **Expected Result:** The user logs in successfully and is redirected to the dashboard.

Other positive test scenarios include:

- Submitting a valid contact form.
- Adding items to a shopping cart and checking out successfully.
- Uploading a supported file format (e.g., uploading a .jpg image when required).

Positive testing ensures that core functionalities work as expected, providing a good user experience.

3. Understanding Negative Test Scenarios

A **negative test scenario** helps determine how an application reacts to invalid or unexpected inputs. This ensures that the system is resilient to errors and prevents crashes or security vulnerabilities.

Example: Testing a Login Page (Negative Scenario)

- **Test Step:** Enter an incorrect password multiple times.
- **Expected Result:** The system displays an error message, and after three failed attempts, the account is temporarily locked.

Other negative test scenarios include:

- Submitting an empty form without filling in required fields.
- Entering an invalid email format (e.g., "user@@domain").
- Uploading an unsupported file type (e.g., .exe instead of .jpg).

Negative testing is essential for identifying weaknesses in input validation and error-handling mechanisms.

4. Best Practices for Designing Positive and Negative Test Scenarios

- **Ensure Comprehensive Coverage** – Include test cases for both expected and unexpected user interactions.
- **Follow Real-World Use Cases** – Simulate how actual users will interact with the system.
- **Use Edge Cases** – Test with extreme values (e.g., very long text inputs, high numerical values).
- **Test Security Aspects** – Ensure the system properly handles invalid inputs without exposing vulnerabilities.
- **Document Expected Results Clearly** – Every test should have a clear success and failure criterion.

Key Takeaway

Both positive and negative test scenarios are critical to software quality assurance. Positive tests confirm that the application functions correctly, while negative tests ensure it handles errors gracefully. A combination of both approaches leads to a robust and user-friendly software product.

In the next section, you'll explore **Boundary Value Analysis and Equivalence Partitioning**, two essential techniques for designing effective test cases.

4.2. Boundary Value Analysis and Equivalence Partitioning

When designing test cases, it is inefficient to test every possible input value. Instead, testers use systematic techniques like **Boundary Value Analysis (BVA)** and **Equivalence Partitioning (EP)** to identify the most important test cases. These techniques help maximize test coverage while minimizing effort.

1. What Is Equivalence Partitioning?

Equivalence Partitioning (EP) is a test case design technique that divides input data into groups (partitions), where each group is expected to behave similarly. Instead of testing every value, you test one representative from each partition.

Example: Testing a Password Length Requirement

Imagine a system that requires a password to be **6 to 12 characters long**.

- **Partition 1 (Invalid):** Passwords **shorter than 6** characters → (e.g., "abc").
- **Partition 2 (Valid):** Passwords between **6 and 12** characters → (e.g., "Test@123").
- **Partition 3 (Invalid):** Passwords **longer than 12** characters → (e.g., "VeryLongPassword123").

Instead of testing every possible password length, you select one test case from each partition:

- A password with **5 characters** (invalid).
- A password with **8 characters** (valid).
- A password with **13 characters** (invalid).

This method reduces redundant testing while ensuring sufficient coverage.

2. What Is Boundary Value Analysis?

Boundary Value Analysis (BVA) focuses on testing values at the edges (boundaries) of valid and invalid input ranges. Since defects often occur at boundaries, testing these values increases the likelihood of finding errors.

Example: Testing an Age Input Field (Valid Range: 18–60)

- **Lower Boundary:** Test **17** (just below valid range) and **18** (minimum valid value).
- **Upper Boundary:** Test **60** (maximum valid value) and **61** (just above valid range).

Test Cases:

- **Valid inputs:** 18, 60
- **Invalid inputs:** 17, 61

By focusing on boundary values, you efficiently uncover defects related to input validation.

3. When to Use EP and BVA?

Technique	When to Use
Equivalence Partitioning	When the input range can be divided into distinct valid and invalid partitions.
Boundary Value Analysis	When testing numerical or ordered data where errors often occur at limits.

Often, both techniques are used together to ensure comprehensive test coverage.

4. Best Practices for Applying EP and BVA

Identify input constraints: Understand the valid and invalid input ranges before designing test cases.
Use minimal test cases: Select representative values to reduce redundancy while maintaining effectiveness.
Combine with other techniques: Pair EP and BVA with **negative testing** to test unexpected inputs.
Consider edge cases: Real-world users often enter values near limits, so thorough boundary testing is essential.

Key Takeaway

Equivalence Partitioning reduces test effort by grouping similar inputs, while **Boundary Value Analysis** ensures edge cases are tested effectively. Together, these techniques help you design efficient and high-impact test cases.

In the next section, you'll explore Common Mistakes in Test Case Design and how to avoid them.

4.3. Common Mistakes in Test Case Design

Designing effective test cases is a critical skill in software testing. However, many testers make common mistakes that reduce test coverage, increase redundancy, or lead to inefficient testing. Understanding these pitfalls can help improve the overall quality of your test cases.

1. Lack of Clear Objectives

Test cases should be written with a clear objective in mind.

- **Mistake:** Writing vague test cases without specifying expected results.
- **Solution:** Clearly define the purpose of each test case and the expected outcome.

2. Poorly Written Test Cases

- **Mistake:** Using ambiguous or unclear language, making it difficult for testers to follow.
- **Solution:** Write test cases in simple, precise, and structured language. Use proper formatting to improve readability.

3. Ignoring Edge Cases and Negative Testing

- **Mistake:** Focusing only on standard or expected inputs, while ignoring edge cases and invalid inputs.
- **Solution:** Include test cases that check boundary values, unexpected inputs, and invalid scenarios.

4. Overlapping or Redundant Test Cases

- **Mistake:** Creating multiple test cases that check the same functionality unnecessarily.
- **Solution:** Optimize test cases by using **Equivalence Partitioning (EP)** and **Boundary Value Analysis (BVA)** to reduce redundancy.

5. Missing Requirement Coverage

- **Mistake:** Not mapping test cases to functional requirements, leading to incomplete testing.
- **Solution:** Use a **Requirement Traceability Matrix (RTM)** to ensure all features are covered.

6. Hardcoding Test Data

- **Mistake:** Using fixed values in test cases instead of parameterizing test data.
- **Solution:** Use **data-driven testing** to allow flexibility and scalability in test execution.

7. Not Prioritizing Test Cases

- **Mistake:** Treating all test cases equally without considering their impact.
- **Solution:** Prioritize test cases based on **business impact, risk, and frequency of use.**

8. Skipping Test Case Reviews

- **Mistake:** Writing and executing test cases without peer review or validation.
- **Solution:** Conduct regular **test case reviews** to identify and fix issues before execution.

9. Lack of Reusability

- **Mistake:** Writing test cases that are too specific and cannot be reused for similar functionalities.
- **Solution:** Design modular and reusable test cases for efficiency and maintainability.

10. Ignoring Automation Feasibility

- **Mistake:** Writing test cases without considering whether they can be automated in the future.

- **Solution:** Design test cases with **automation compatibility** in mind, using structured and well-defined steps.

Key Takeaway

Avoiding these common mistakes will help you write **clear, effective, and efficient** test cases that improve software quality. Always focus on **clarity, coverage, efficiency, and reusability** when designing test cases.

In the next chapter, you will explore Test Case Management, including tools and strategies for organizing and maintaining test cases effectively.

4.4. Organizing Test Cases for Maximum Efficiency

Effective test case organization is essential for maintaining structured and scalable testing efforts. Without proper organization, test cases become difficult to manage, leading to inefficiencies, duplication, and gaps in test coverage.

This section provides **best practices** for organizing test cases in a way that enhances efficiency, collaboration, and maintainability.

1. Why Test Case Organization Matters

Proper organization of test cases helps you:

- **Improve Test Coverage:** Ensure all functionalities are tested without redundancy.
- **Enhance Productivity:** Reduce time spent searching for and managing test cases.
- **Streamline Execution:** Enable testers to quickly identify and execute relevant tests.
- **Facilitate Reusability:** Allow easy reuse of test cases for future projects.
- **Support Collaboration:** Make test cases understandable and accessible to all team members.

2. Structuring Test Cases Efficiently

To maximize efficiency, follow these structured approaches when organizing test cases:

a. Categorize Test Cases Based on Functionality

- **Module-Based Organization:** Group test cases by software modules or features.
- **User Scenario-Based Organization:** Structure test cases based on end-user workflows.
- **Business-Critical vs. Non-Critical Tests:** Prioritize essential test cases to focus on high-impact functionalities.

b. Use a Standard Naming Convention

i. Create **clear and descriptive** test case names to make them easily identifiable.

ii. Example format:

- `[Module]_[Feature]_[Scenario]_[ExpectedOutcome]`
- **Example:** `Login_InvalidPassword_ErrorMessageDisplayed`

c. Implement a Test Case ID System

i. Assign **unique identifiers** to test cases for easy tracking.

ii. Example: `TC001, TC002, TC003`, etc.

iii. Use a **hierarchical structure** if needed, such as:

- `MOD1_TC001` (Module 1, Test Case 1)
- `MOD2_TC002` (Module 2, Test Case 2)

d. Organize Test Cases by Priority

- **High Priority:** Critical functionalities that must work correctly.
- **Medium Priority:** Important but non-critical features.

- **Low Priority:** Optional features or enhancements.

e. Group Test Cases by Test Type

- **Functional Tests:** Validate that software behaves as expected.
- **Regression Tests:** Ensure new changes do not break existing features.
- **Smoke Tests:** Quick checks to confirm system stability before in-depth testing.
- **Performance Tests:** Evaluate system speed, responsiveness, and load capacity.
- **Security Tests:** Identify vulnerabilities in the system.

f. Establish Clear Test Case Statuses

Track progress efficiently by assigning test cases one of the following statuses:

- **Not Executed:** The test case has not been run yet.
- **Passed:** The test case executed successfully with expected results.
- **Failed:** The test case failed due to a defect.
- **Blocked:** The test case could not be executed due to dependencies or issues.
- **Retest:** The test needs to be re-executed after a fix.

3. Best Practices for Organizing Test Cases

Follow these best practices to maintain an **efficient and scalable** test case repository:

- **Use Test Case Management Tools:** Leverage tools like **Jira, TestRail, qTest**, or **TestLink** to store, manage, and execute test cases.
- **Keep Test Cases Concise and Focused:** Each test case should verify a specific functionality **without excessive steps**.
- **Ensure Reusability:** Write modular test cases that can be reused across multiple test scenarios.

- **Maintain Version Control:** Track changes to test cases to ensure they stay up-to-date with software updates.
- **Regularly Review and Optimize:** Periodically review test cases to remove duplicates, outdated tests, or unnecessary steps.

4. Example: Organizing Test Cases in a Test Management Tool

Here's how you can structure your test cases in **TestRail** or **Jira**:

1. Create Test Suites:

- **Suite 1:** Login & Authentication
- **Suite 2:** User Profile Management
- **Suite 3:** Payment Processing

2. Within Each Suite, Create Sections:

- **Positive Scenarios**
- **Negative Scenarios**
- **Boundary Value Tests**

3. Use Tags and Filters for Easy Retrieval:

Example tags: `#Regression, #Critical, #API_Testing, #UI_Testing`

By following this structured approach, you ensure **faster execution, improved test coverage, and streamlined test management**.

Key Takeaway

Organizing test cases effectively saves time, enhances collaboration, and improves test execution efficiency. By implementing **clear naming conventions, prioritization, categorization, and management tools**, you can maintain a well-structured test case repository that scales with your project.

In the next section, you’ll learn how to **create and manage test suites** for even better test organization.

5. Test Case Management

5.1. Using Test Case Management Tools (Jira, TestRail, etc.)

Managing test cases effectively is essential for ensuring structured and efficient software testing. Test Case Management (TCM) tools help QA teams organize, execute, and track test cases, making it easier to manage testing efforts across projects.

1. What Are Test Case Management Tools?

Test Case Management tools are specialized software platforms designed to:

- Store and organize test cases in a structured manner.
- Track test execution progress and results.
- Assign test cases to testers and track responsibility.
- Generate reports for stakeholders.
- Integrate with issue-tracking tools like Jira to streamline bug reporting.

2. Popular Test Case Management Tools

i. Jira (With Xray or Zephyr Plug-ins)

Overview:

Jira is primarily an issue-tracking tool, but it supports test case management through plugins like Xray and Zephyr.

Key Features:

- Create and link test cases to user stories or issues.
- Plan and execute test cycles.
- Generate detailed test reports.
- Integrate with automation tools like Selenium.

Best For:

Teams already using Jira for development and issue tracking.

ii. TestRail

Overview:

A comprehensive test management tool designed for structured test case organization.

Key Features:

- Intuitive dashboard for tracking test progress.
- Supports both manual and automated test cases.
- Integration with Jira, Selenium, and CI/CD tools.
- Customizable reporting and analytics.

Best For:

Medium to large teams needing a dedicated test management system.

iii. qTest (by Tricentis)

Overview:

An enterprise-grade test management tool designed for Agile and DevOps teams.

Key Features:

- Advanced test case tracking and analytics.
- CI/CD and automation integration.
- Scalable for enterprise-level projects.

Best For:

Large organizations with complex test management needs.

iv. TestLink

Overview:

A free and open-source test management tool for teams looking for a cost-effective solution.

Key Features:

- Web-based interface for test case management.
- Supports test execution tracking.
- Integrates with issue-tracking tools.

Best For:

Small teams and projects with budget constraints.

3. Key Benefits of Using Test Case Management Tools

- **Improved Organization:** Centralized test repository for easy access.
- **Better Collaboration:** Enables testers, developers, and managers to work efficiently.
- **Faster Execution:** Streamlines test planning and execution workflows.
- **Enhanced Reporting:** Generates insights into test progress and software quality.
- **Integration with Automation:** Seamlessly connects with automation frameworks.

4. Choosing the Right Test Case Management Tool

When selecting a TCM tool, consider the following factors:

- **Project Size and Complexity:** Large projects may need advanced features, while smaller teams can opt for simpler solutions.
- **Integration Needs:** Ensure the tool integrates with your existing development and automation tools.
- **Budget:** Open-source tools like TestLink are free, while enterprise

solutions like qTest may require licensing fees.
- **Ease of Use:** The tool should be user-friendly for efficient adoption by the team.

Key Takeaway

Test Case Management tools play a crucial role in organizing and executing test cases effectively. By choosing the right tool, QA teams can improve productivity, ensure better test coverage, and enhance collaboration.

In the next section, you'll learn about **how to organize test cases for maximum efficiency** to streamline your testing workflow.

5.2. Organizing Test Cases for Maximum Efficiency

Effective test case organization is essential for maintaining structured and scalable testing efforts. Without proper organization, test cases become difficult to manage, leading to inefficiencies, duplication, and gaps in test coverage.

This section provides **best practices** for organizing test cases in a way that enhances efficiency, collaboration, and maintainability.

1. Why Test Case Organization Matters

Proper organization of test cases helps you:

- **Improve Test Coverage:** Ensure all functionalities are tested without redundancy.
- **Enhance Productivity:** Reduce time spent searching for and managing test cases.
- **Streamline Execution:** Enable testers to quickly identify and execute relevant tests.
- **Facilitate Reusability:** Allow easy reuse of test cases for future projects.
- **Support Collaboration:** Make test cases understandable and accessible to all team members.

2. Structuring Test Cases Efficiently

To maximize efficiency, follow these structured approaches when organizing test cases:

a. Categorize Test Cases Based on Functionality

- **Module-Based Organization:** Group test cases by software modules or features.
- **User Scenario-Based Organization:** Structure test cases based on end-user workflows.
- **Business-Critical vs. Non-Critical Tests:** Prioritize essential test cases to focus on high-impact functionalities.

b. Use a Standard Naming Convention

i. Create **clear and descriptive** test case names to make them easily identifiable.

ii. Example format:

- [Module]_[Feature]_[Scenario]_[ExpectedOutcome]
- **Example:** Login_InvalidPassword_ErrorMessageDisplayed

c. Implement a Test Case ID System

i. Assign **unique identifiers** to test cases for easy tracking.

ii. Example: TC001, TC002, TC003, etc.

iii. Use a **hierarchical structure** if needed, such as:

- `MOD1_TC001` (Module 1, Test Case 1)
- `MOD2_TC002` (Module 2, Test Case 2)

d. Organize Test Cases by Priority

- **High Priority:** Critical functionalities that must work correctly.

- **Medium Priority:** Important but non-critical features.
- **Low Priority:** Optional features or enhancements.

e. Group Test Cases by Test Type

- **Functional Tests:** Validate that software behaves as expected.
- **Regression Tests:** Ensure new changes do not break existing features.
- **Smoke Tests:** Quick checks to confirm system stability before in-depth testing.
- **Performance Tests:** Evaluate system speed, responsiveness, and load capacity.
- **Security Tests:** Identify vulnerabilities in the system.

f. Establish Clear Test Case Statuses

Track progress efficiently by assigning test cases one of the following statuses:

- **Not Executed:** The test case has not been run yet.
- **Passed:** The test case executed successfully with expected results.
- **Failed:** The test case failed due to a defect.
- **Blocked:** The test case could not be executed due to dependencies or issues.
- **Retest:** The test needs to be re-executed after a fix.

3. Best Practices for Organizing Test Cases

Follow these best practices to maintain an **efficient and scalable** test case repository:

- **Use Test Case Management Tools:** Leverage tools like **Jira, TestRail, qTest**, or **TestLink** to store, manage, and execute test cases.
- **Keep Test Cases Concise and Focused:** Each test case should verify a specific functionality **without excessive steps**.
- **Ensure Reusability:** Write modular test cases that can be reused

across multiple test scenarios.

- **Maintain Version Control:** Track changes to test cases to ensure they stay up-to-date with software updates.
- **Regularly Review and Optimize:** Periodically review test cases to remove duplicates, outdated tests, or unnecessary steps.

4. Example: Organizing Test Cases in a Test Management Tool

Here's how you can structure your test cases in **TestRail** or **Jira**:

i. Create Test Suites:

- **Suite 1:** Login & Authentication
- **Suite 2:** User Profile Management
- **Suite 3:** Payment Processing

ii. Within Each Suite, Create Sections:

- **Positive Scenarios**
- **Negative Scenarios**
- **Boundary Value Tests**

iii. Use Tags and Filters for Easy Retrieval:

- Example tags: `#Regression`, `#Critical`, `#API_Testing`, `#UI_Testing`

By following this structured approach, you ensure **faster execution, improved test coverage, and streamlined test management**.

Key Takeaway

Organizing test cases effectively saves time, enhances collaboration, and improves test execution efficiency. By implementing **clear naming conventions, prioritization, categorization, and management tools**, you can maintain a well-structured test case repository that scales with your project.

In the next section, you'll learn how to **create and manage test suites** for even better test organization.

5.3. Creating and Managing Test Suites

Test suites play a crucial role in organizing and executing test cases efficiently. A **test suite** is a collection of related test cases grouped together to validate specific functionalities, modules, or scenarios within a software application. Properly structured test suites ensure **better test coverage, easier execution, and improved test management.**

This section will guide you through **creating, organizing, and managing test suites effectively** using best practices and test management tools like **Jira, TestRail, qTest, and TestLink.**

1. Understanding Test Suites

A **test suite** consists of multiple test cases that share a common objective. It can be categorized based on:

- **Software modules** (e.g., Login, Checkout, User Profile)
- **Testing types** (e.g., Regression, Smoke, Performance)
- **User scenarios** (e.g., New User Registration, Returning Customer Purchase)
- **Priority levels** (e.g., Critical, High, Medium, Low)

Properly structuring your test suites helps streamline execution and ensures that **no critical functionality is overlooked.**

2. Steps to Create a Well-Organized Test Suite

Step 1: Define the Purpose of the Test Suite

Before creating a test suite, determine its objective:

- **What functionality or feature does it test?**
- **Is it for regression, smoke, or functional testing?**
- **Does it focus on a specific user journey?**

Clearly defining the purpose ensures that the suite remains focused and relevant.

Step 2: Organize Test Cases Logically

Group test cases based on logical criteria to enhance readability and execution efficiency:

- **Module-based grouping:** Group test cases by software module (e.g., Login, Payments).
- **Scenario-based grouping:** Organize by user journey (e.g., First-time login, Checkout process).
- **Priority-based grouping:** Ensure high-priority tests are executed first.
- **Test type-based grouping:** Separate functional, performance, regression, and security test cases.

Step 3: Assign a Unique Test Suite Name and ID

Use a standardized naming convention to make test suites easy to track. A good format is:

- `[ProjectName]_[Module]_[TestType]_[SuiteNumber]`
- **Example:** `Ecommerce_Login_Functional_TS01`

Step 4: Include Detailed Descriptions

Each test suite should have a **clear description** outlining:

- **Scope:** What the test suite covers.
- **Dependencies:** Any prerequisites before execution.
- **Expected Outcome:** The anticipated results after execution.

Step 5: Add Relevant Test Cases

Once your suite is created, add test cases that align with its purpose. Ensure:

- No duplicate test cases are added.
- Test cases are well-structured and easy to execute.
- Each test case follows a standard format (e.g., ID, Title, Steps, Expected Result).

3. Best Practices for Managing Test Suites

To keep your test suites efficient and up to date, follow these best practices:

a. Regularly Review and Update Test Suites

- Remove obsolete test cases that no longer apply to the application.
- Update test cases when application functionality changes.
- Ensure test cases **align with new requirements** or feature updates.

b. Leverage Test Suite Versioning

- Maintain different versions of test suites to track changes over time.
- Example: `Login_Regression_TS_v1, Login_Regression_TS_v2`.

c. Use Tags and Filters for Easy Management

- Apply tags like `#Critical, #UI_Testing, #Performance` to make searching easier.
- Use filters in test management tools to retrieve specific test suites quickly.

d. Optimize Execution Order

- Prioritize test suites based on risk and importance.
- Run **high-priority and smoke tests first** before deeper testing.
- Execute **automation-compatible test suites** in parallel for efficiency.

e. Assign Test Suites to Specific Teams or Testers

- Distribute ownership of test suites among team members.
- Clearly define **who is responsible** for updating and executing each

suite.

4. Using Test Management Tools for Test Suites

Jira + Xray

- Create test suites using **Xray's "Test Set" feature.**
- Link related test cases to **track execution status in Jira dashboards.**

TestRail

- Organize test suites within **test runs** for systematic execution.
- Use filters and tagging to **retrieve specific test scenarios easily.**

qTest

- Manage test suites in a **hierarchical structure** with folders and labels.
- Track real-time execution results for **better visibility into testing progress.**

TestLink

- Define and maintain test suites **with built-in version control.**
- Integrate with automation tools for **seamless test execution.**

5. Example of a Well-Structured Test Suite in TestRail

Test Suite Name: `Ecommerce_Checkout_Regression_TS01`

Description: Tests the checkout process for both registered and guest users.

Test Case ID	Test Case Name	Priority	Status
TC001	Validate guest checkout process	High	Not Executed
TC002	Verify payment success page	Critical	Passed
TC003	Ensure discount codes apply correctly	Medium	Failed

By structuring your test suites this way, you ensure **clarity, efficiency, and easy maintenance.**

Key Takeaway

Creating and managing test suites properly enhances test organization, execution efficiency, and software quality. By using **logical grouping, standard naming conventions, test management tools, and regular updates**, you can **streamline testing efforts** and improve overall productivity.

In the next chapter, you'll learn about **executing test cases and logging defects effectively.**

6. Test Execution and Bug Reporting

6.1. How to Execute Manual Test Cases

Executing manual test cases is a crucial step in the software testing process. It involves following predefined test steps, comparing expected and actual results, and reporting any deviations as defects. Proper execution ensures software functionality, reliability, and user satisfaction.

This section will guide you through the **best practices, step-by-step execution process, and common challenges** in manual test execution.

1. Understanding Manual Test Execution

Manual test execution involves:

- Running test cases without using automation tools to validate software functionality.
- Following detailed test steps to check expected vs. actual behavior.
- Identifying, documenting, and reporting bugs for further investigation.
- Ensuring that software meets business requirements and user expectations.

You should execute test cases **systematically and accurately** to maintain software quality.

2. Steps to Execute Manual Test Cases

Step 1: Prepare for Test Execution

Before running test cases, ensure the following:

- **Test environment is ready:** Confirm that hardware, software, databases, and network settings are properly configured.
- **Test data is available:** Prepare required input values (e.g., usernames, passwords, test product data).

- **Test cases are updated:** Ensure all test cases are current and reflect the latest system changes.
- **Required tools are accessible:** Have access to defect tracking tools (e.g., Jira, Bugzilla) and documentation tools (e.g., Confluence, TestRail).

Step 2: Execute Test Cases Systematically

- **Follow test case steps carefully:** Perform actions exactly as outlined.
- **Check expected vs. actual results:** Compare actual system behavior with predefined expected outcomes.
- **Log observations:** Note any unusual behavior, UI glitches, or unexpected responses.
- **Capture evidence:** Take screenshots or screen recordings if necessary.

Step 3: Validate Pass/Fail Criteria

Each test case must be marked as:

- **Pass:** If the actual result matches the expected result.
- **Fail:** If there is any deviation from the expected outcome.
- **Blocked:** If an issue prevents execution (e.g., system crash, missing permissions).
- **Not Executed:** If the test case has not been run yet.

Step 4: Document and Report Defects

- Record failed test cases with clear descriptions.
- Provide **steps to reproduce the bug** for developers.
- Attach logs, error messages, and screenshots for better analysis.
- Assign severity and priority to each defect (e.g., **Critical, High, Medium, Low**).

Step 5: Retest and Verify Fixes

- After developers fix defects, **re-execute failed test cases** to verify the resolution.
- Ensure the fix does not introduce new bugs (Regression Testing).
- Update the test case status accordingly.

3. Best Practices for Effective Test Execution

To improve efficiency and accuracy, follow these best practices:

a. Execute in a Structured Manner

- Follow a **logical sequence** instead of random execution.
- Prioritize **critical test cases** before less important ones.
- Use a **test execution checklist** to track progress.

b. Maintain Detailed Test Logs

- Document **execution date, tester name, environment details, and test results.**
- Capture **edge cases and unexpected behavior** for future reference.

c. Communicate Clearly with the Team

- Inform developers and stakeholders of critical defects immediately.
- Collaborate with other testers to share findings and insights.

d. Use a Test Management Tool

- Store and track execution results using tools like **TestRail, qTest, or Zephyr.**
- Link test cases to requirements and defects for traceability.

e. Perform Exploratory Testing Alongside Scripted Testing

- Go beyond predefined steps to identify hidden issues.
- Test **edge cases, error handling, and usability aspects.**

4. Common Challenges in Manual Test Execution and How to Overcome Them

Challenge	Solution
Test case ambiguity	Ensure test cases have clear and detailed steps.
Time constraints	Prioritize test cases based on risk and impact.
Environment issues	Work with the DevOps team to maintain stability.
Lack of test data	Create diverse test datasets before execution.
Flaky test results	Retest and confirm before reporting defects.

5. Example: Manual Test Execution Log

Test Case ID	Test Case Name	Steps Executed	Expected Result	Actual Result	Status	Remarks
TC001	Login with valid credentials	Enter username & password, click login	Dashboard loads successfully	Dashboard loads	Pass	N/A

TC002	Login with incorrect password	Enter wrong password, click login	Error message displayed	No error message	Fail	Reported bug #123
TC003	Checkout process validation	Add product, enter details, place order	Order confirmation received	Payment gateway crashes	Fail	Critical bug reported

Key Takeaway

Executing manual test cases requires attention to detail, clear documentation, and effective defect reporting. By following structured execution steps, best practices, and leveraging test management tools, you can enhance software quality and ensure a smooth testing process.

In the next section, you'll learn how to **identify and log bugs properly for efficient debugging and resolution.**

6.2. Identifying and Logging Bugs Properly

Effective bug identification and logging are crucial for **ensuring software quality, improving development efficiency, and minimizing defects in production.** Poorly documented bugs can lead to **delays, miscommunication, and unresolved issues.**

This section will guide you on how to **identify, categorize, and log defects properly** so developers can resolve them efficiently.

1. Understanding Bug Identification

A **bug** (also called a defect) is any **unexpected behavior, deviation from requirements, or system failure** that impacts the software's functionality, performance, security, or usability.

Common Types of Bugs

- **Functional Bugs** – Features not working as expected (e.g., login failure, incorrect calculations).
- **UI/UX Bugs** – Misalignment, broken elements, inconsistent design, or poor user experience.
- **Performance Issues** – Slow response time, memory leaks, or excessive resource consumption.
- **Security Vulnerabilities** – Weak authentication, data exposure, or SQL injection risks.
- **Compatibility Issues** – Inconsistencies across browsers, devices, or operating systems.
- **Integration Bugs** – Failures in API communication, third-party service interactions, or database operations.

You must **thoroughly analyze** software behavior to confirm whether an issue is truly a bug before logging it.

2. Steps to Identify Bugs Effectively

Step 1: Understand the Requirements

- Review functional specifications and user stories to understand expected behavior.
- Cross-check with **business rules, design documents, and acceptance criteria.**

Step 2: Observe and Analyze System Behavior

- Run the test case and compare **actual results vs. expected results.**
- Observe **unexpected errors, UI glitches, incorrect outputs, or system crashes.**
- Check browser console logs, network requests, and system logs for hidden issues.

Step 3: Reproduce the Bug

- Perform the same steps multiple times to confirm it is not a one-time occurrence.
- Try different **input values, user roles, and device configurations** to check consistency.
- If the issue is intermittent, try capturing error logs or using debugging tools.

Step 4: Categorize the Bug

a. Severity Levels:

- **Critical:** System crash, security breach, or data loss.
- **High:** Major functionality failure, blocking user actions.
- **Medium:** Partial feature failure, workarounds available.
- **Low:** Minor UI issues, typos, or cosmetic defects.

b. Priority Levels:

- **High:** Needs immediate fixing due to major impact.
- **Medium:** Can be addressed in the next release.
- **Low:** Does not impact core functionality but should be fixed later.

3. How to Log Bugs Properly

Once you identify a bug, you must log it **clearly and precisely** in a defect tracking system like **Jira, Bugzilla, Trello, or Azure DevOps.**

Bug Report Template

Field	**Description**
Bug ID	Auto-generated unique identifier.

Title	A short, descriptive summary of the issue.
Description	A detailed explanation of the bug, expected vs. actual behavior.
Steps to Reproduce	Clear step-by-step instructions to replicate the issue.
Environment	OS, browser version, device, test environment details.
Severity	Impact level (Critical, High, Medium, Low).
Priority	Urgency level (High, Medium, Low).
Attachments	Screenshots, logs, video recordings, or error messages.
Assigned To	Developer responsible for fixing the issue.
Status	Open, In Progress, Resolved, Closed.

Example Bug Report (Jira Format)

Title:

Login Page – "Forgot Password" Link Not Working

Description:

The "Forgot Password" link on the login page does not redirect users to the password reset page. Instead, it reloads the login page.

Steps to Reproduce:

1. Open the application login page.
2. Click on the **"Forgot Password"** link.
3. Observe that the page reloads instead of navigating to the reset page.

Expected Result:

User should be redirected to the password reset page to enter their email.

Actual Result:

Clicking on the "Forgot Password" link reloads the login page.

Environment:

- **OS:** Windows 11
- **Browser:** Chrome 119.0.1234.56
- **Device:** Desktop
- **Test Environment:** Staging

Severity:

Medium

Priority:

High

Attachments:

(Attach screenshot or video recording)

4. Best Practices for Effective Bug Logging

a. Be Clear and Concise

- Use **specific, actionable language.** Avoid vague descriptions like *"Not working"* or *"Something is broken."*

- Example: Instead of *"Button doesn't work,"* write *"Submit button does not respond when clicked on Chrome (v119)."*

b. Include Step-by-Step Instructions

- Provide **exact steps** so developers can easily reproduce the issue.
- Use numbered steps for clarity.

c. Provide Expected vs. Actual Behavior

- Clearly define what **should happen** versus what actually happens.

d. Attach Evidence (Screenshots, Logs, Videos)

- Use **screenshots** with annotations to highlight the issue.
- Attach **error logs** or console outputs for debugging.
- Record **screen videos** for complex issues.

e. Categorize and Prioritize Correctly

- Assign **appropriate severity and priority** to help teams address critical bugs first.

f. Keep the Bug Report Updated

- Change the status as the issue progresses (*Open → In Progress → Fixed → Closed*).
- Add **developer comments** if additional information is needed.

5. Common Mistakes to Avoid in Bug Logging

Mistake	Solution
Vague bug descriptions	Be specific. Clearly state the issue and impact.

Missing reproduction steps	Provide detailed step-by-step instructions.
No evidence attached	Always attach logs, screenshots, or videos.
Wrong severity or priority	Assess impact properly before assigning levels.
Not checking for duplicates	Search for similar bugs before logging a new one.

Key Takeaway

Proper bug identification and logging are essential for effective debugging, smooth software development, and high-quality product releases. By following structured bug logging practices, using defect tracking tools, and providing clear documentation, you ensure that issues are resolved efficiently.

In the next section, you'll learn how to **write effective bug reports with detailed steps, evidence, and prioritization strategies.**

6.3. Writing Effective Bug Reports (Steps to Reproduce, Screenshots, etc.)

A well-documented bug report helps developers quickly understand, reproduce, and fix defects without unnecessary back-and-forth communication. Poorly written reports can delay bug resolution, lead to misunderstandings, or even cause critical issues to be ignored.

In this section, you'll learn **how to structure an effective bug report** that contains all necessary details to streamline the debugging process.

1. Key Components of an Effective Bug Report

A high-quality bug report should **clearly and concisely describe the issue, its impact, and how to reproduce it.** Every bug report should include:

- **Title** – A short, descriptive summary of the issue.
- **Description** – A detailed explanation of the bug and its impact.
- **Steps to Reproduce** – Clear step-by-step instructions to replicate the issue.
- **Expected vs. Actual Results** – What should happen vs. what actually happens.
- **Environment Details** – OS, browser, device, application version, etc.
- **Severity & Priority** – How critical and urgent the bug is.
- **Attachments** – Screenshots, logs, error messages, or video recordings.
- **Status & Assignee** – The current progress of the issue and who is responsible.

2. How to Write a Clear Bug Report

Step 1: Write a Clear and Specific Bug Title

The title should **summarize the problem in one sentence** so it's easy to understand at a glance.

Example of a Good Bug Title:

"Login Page – 'Forgot Password' Link Reloads the Page Instead of Redirecting to Reset Screen"

Example of a Bad Bug Title:

"Forgot Password not working"

Step 2: Provide a Detailed Bug Description

Clearly explain **what the bug is, where it occurs, and its impact on the system.**

Example:

"The 'Forgot Password' link on the login page does not take users to the password reset screen. Instead, clicking the link reloads the login page, preventing users from recovering their password. This issue occurs in Chrome (v119) and Firefox (v118) but works fine in Safari (v16)."

Step 3: List Steps to Reproduce the Bug

Developers need **precise instructions** to replicate the issue. Use **numbered steps** to provide a structured flow.

Example:

1. Open the application login page.
2. Click on the **"Forgot Password"** link below the password field.
3. Observe that the page reloads instead of navigating to the password reset screen.

Step 4: Define Expected vs. Actual Results

Clearly state **what should happen** versus **what actually happens** to highlight the deviation.

Example:

Expected Result	**Actual Result**
Clicking the "Forgot Password" link should navigate to the password reset page.	The page reloads instead of redirecting to the reset screen.

Step 5: Specify the Environment Details

Bugs can behave differently in various environments. Always include:

- **Operating System** (Windows 11, macOS Ventura, Android 13, etc.)
- **Browser & Version** (Chrome 119, Firefox 118, Safari 16, etc.)
- **Device Type** (Desktop, iPhone 14, Samsung Galaxy S23, etc.)
- **Test Environment** (Staging, Production, Dev, etc.)

Example:

- **OS:** Windows 11
- **Browser:** Chrome 119.0.1234.56
- **Device:** Desktop
- **Test Environment:** Staging

Step 6: Assign Severity and Priority Levels

Understanding the **impact and urgency** helps teams prioritize bug fixes effectively.

Severity Levels:

- **Critical** – System crash, security vulnerability, or data loss.
- **High** – Major feature failure, blocking core functionality.
- **Medium** – Partial feature failure, but workarounds available.
- **Low** – Minor UI issues, typos, or cosmetic bugs.

Priority Levels:

- **High** – Must be fixed immediately due to major impact.
- **Medium** – Can be addressed in the next release.
- **Low** – Does not require immediate attention.

Step 7: Attach Screenshots, Logs, or Videos

- **Screenshots:** Highlight the issue visually. Use **annotations** (arrows, boxes) to pinpoint problems.
- **Videos:** If the bug involves **animations, multi-step processes, or intermittent issues,** record a short video.
- **Error Logs:** Attach **console logs, API response errors, or system**

logs for backend issues.

Example Screenshot Annotation:

"Redirection issue when clicking 'Forgot Password' link in Chrome v119" (See attached screenshot: bug_screenshot.png)

3. Example of a Well-Written Bug Report

Title:

"Login Page – 'Forgot Password' Link Reloads Instead of Redirecting to Reset Screen"

Description:

The 'Forgot Password' link on the login page does not take users to the password reset screen. Instead, clicking the link reloads the login page. This prevents users from recovering their password. The issue occurs in Chrome (v119) and Firefox (v118) but works correctly in Safari (v16).

Steps to Reproduce:

1. Open the application login page.
2. Click on the **"Forgot Password"** link.
3. Observe that the page reloads instead of navigating to the reset screen.

Expected vs. Actual Results:

Expected Result	Actual Result
Clicking the "Forgot Password" link should navigate to the password reset page.	The page reloads instead of redirecting to the reset screen.

Environment Details:

- **OS:** Windows 11
- **Browser:** Chrome 119.0.1234.56
- **Device:** Desktop
- **Test Environment:** Staging

Severity & Priority:

- **Severity:** Medium
- **Priority:** High

Attachments:

- Screenshot: bug_screenshot.png
- Console Log: error_log.txt
- Video: bug_demo.mp4

Status: Open

Assigned To: [Developer's Name]

4. Best Practices for Writing Effective Bug Reports

Be Precise and Specific

- Avoid vague descriptions like *"Form doesn't work"* – specify *what isn't working and under what conditions.*
- Use structured formats to **clearly document issues.**

Reproduce the Issue Before Logging

- **Confirm the bug is consistent** and not a one-time error.
- Check if the issue occurs **across different browsers, devices, or environments.**

Use Screenshots and Videos for Clarity

- Highlight **specific errors, misalignments, or UI glitches.**
- Provide **step-by-step screen recordings for complex issues.**

Categorize the Bug Properly

- **Assign correct severity and priority** so critical issues are addressed first.
- If unsure, **consult with team members** before assigning levels.

Check for Duplicate Bugs

- **Search the bug tracking system** before logging a new issue to avoid duplicates.

Update Bug Status Regularly

- Track progress using **statuses like Open, In Progress, Fixed, and Closed.**
- Add **comments or updates** if additional testing is required.

Key Takeaway

A well-written bug report saves time, improves communication, and speeds up resolution. By following a structured approach, including clear steps to reproduce, environment details, and supporting evidence, you ensure that developers can quickly identify and fix defects.

In the next section, you'll learn about **common bug tracking tools like Jira and Bugzilla and how to use them effectively.**

6.4. Common Bug Tracking Tools (Jira, Bugzilla, etc.)

Bug tracking tools play a crucial role in identifying, documenting, and managing software defects throughout the development lifecycle. Using an efficient bug tracking system improves collaboration between testers, developers, and project managers, ensuring that bugs are properly logged, assigned, and resolved in a structured manner.

In this section, you will learn about **popular bug tracking tools**, their **key features**, and **how to choose the right tool for your team.**

1. Why Use Bug Tracking Tools?

Manual tracking of defects through spreadsheets or emails **is inefficient and prone to errors.** Bug tracking tools provide:

- **Centralized Bug Management** – All bugs are stored and tracked in one place.
- **Better Collaboration** – Developers, testers, and managers can communicate efficiently.
- **Automated Notifications** – Team members receive updates on bug status changes.
- **Custom Workflow Management** – Bugs follow a defined life cycle (Open → In Progress → Fixed → Verified).
- **Integration with Other Tools** – Many bug trackers integrate with test management and development tools like GitHub, Jenkins, and Selenium.

2. Popular Bug Tracking Tools

1. Jira

Jira is a widely used bug tracking and project management tool developed by Atlassian.

Key Features:

- **Issue Tracking:** Log, prioritize, and assign bugs efficiently.
- **Custom Workflows:** Define unique workflows for your team.
- **Agile Boards:** Supports Scrum and Kanban boards for tracking progress.
- **Automation:** Automate tasks like bug assignment and status updates.

- **Integration:** Works with tools like Confluence, Bitbucket, GitHub, and Slack.

Best For:

- Teams following **Agile, Scrum, or Kanban methodologies**.
- Large teams managing **complex projects**.

Limitations:

- Steep learning curve for beginners.
- Can be **expensive for small teams**.

2. Bugzilla

Bugzilla is an open-source bug tracking system developed by Mozilla. It is known for its **simplicity and efficiency** in managing defects.

Key Features:

- **Advanced Search and Filtering:** Quickly locate specific bugs.
- **Email Notifications:** Get notified of bug status updates.
- **Custom Fields:** Adapt bug reports to your project needs.
- **Security Controls:** Restrict access to confidential bugs.

Best For:

- **Small to medium-sized teams** that need a **free and efficient** bug tracking solution.
- Organizations looking for a **lightweight, open-source alternative**.

Limitations:

- **Outdated interface** compared to modern tools.
- Lacks **native integration** with project management software.

3. Trello

Trello is a **simple, visual project management tool** that can also be used for bug tracking.

Key Features:

- **Kanban-style boards** for organizing bug reports.
- **Drag-and-drop functionality** for easy bug tracking.
- **Custom Labels & Tags** to categorize issues.
- **Integration with Slack, GitHub, and Jira**.

Best For:

- Small teams or startups with **simple bug tracking needs**.
- **Non-technical users** who prefer a visual approach.

Limitations:

- Lacks **advanced bug tracking features** like custom workflows and detailed reporting.
- Not ideal for **complex software development projects**.

4. Redmine

Redmine is an **open-source project management and bug tracking tool** with a flexible, web-based interface.

Key Features:

- **Multi-project support** with role-based access control.
- **Gantt charts and calendars** for tracking progress.
- **Time tracking and reporting** for bug fixes.
- **Integration with version control systems** like Git and SVN.

Best For:

- **Teams that need a self-hosted solution** with **customization options**.
- **Development teams using version control tools** for code tracking.

Limitations:

- Requires **technical expertise to set up and maintain**.
- User interface is **less modern** than Jira or Trello.

5. MantisBT

Mantis Bug Tracker (MantisBT) is an **open-source bug tracking system** that is easy to set up and use.

Key Features:

- **Email notifications** for bug updates.
- **Customizable access control** for different users.
- **Plugin support** to extend functionalities.
- **Mobile-friendly interface** for tracking bugs on the go.

Best For:

- **Teams looking for a free, lightweight bug tracker**.
- Organizations that want a **simple alternative to Bugzilla**.

Limitations:

- **Basic UI compared to Jira and other modern tools**.
- Lacks **advanced Agile project management features**.

3. How to Choose the Right Bug Tracking Tool

When selecting a bug tracking tool, consider the following factors:

a. Team Size and Needs

- For **large teams with complex workflows**, use **Jira or Bugzilla**.
- For **small teams or startups**, use **Trello or MantisBT**.

b. Budget

- **Bugzilla, Redmine, and MantisBT** are **free and open-source**.

- **Jira and Trello** have **paid plans** with advanced features.

c. Integration with Other Tools

- If you use **CI/CD tools (Jenkins, GitHub, GitLab)**, choose a bug tracker that integrates well with them.
- If using **Agile project management**, Jira is the best option.

d. Ease of Use

- **Trello** is the easiest to use, but lacks advanced bug tracking features.
- **Jira and Bugzilla** offer more power but have a **steeper learning curve**.

e. Hosting Options

- **Self-hosted:** Bugzilla, Redmine, MantisBT.
- **Cloud-based:** Jira, Trello.

4. Best Practices for Using Bug Tracking Tools

- **Standardize Bug Reporting:** Ensure all team members follow a consistent format when logging bugs.
- **Assign Clear Ownership:** Every bug should have a designated **assignee** and **priority level**.
- **Use Labels & Categories:** Group bugs by **severity, feature, or sprint cycle** for better organization.
- **Regularly Review Bug Reports:** Schedule **bug triage meetings** to prioritize and address defects.
- **Integrate with Version Control:** If using **GitHub, GitLab, or Bitbucket**, link bug reports to code changes.
- **Automate Notifications:** Set up **email or Slack notifications** for bug status updates.

Key Takeaway

Using a **bug tracking tool** improves **efficiency, collaboration, and defect resolution** in software projects. Jira, Bugzilla, and Redmine are great for

structured bug management, while Trello and MantisBT are ideal for **simpler workflows. Choose a tool based on your team's size, budget, and project complexity.**

In the next chapter, you'll learn about **the fundamentals of automated testing and its role in software quality assurance.**

Part 3: Transitioning from Manual to Automated Testing

7. Introduction to Automation in QA

7.1. What is Test Automation?

As software applications become more complex, manual testing alone is often insufficient to meet the growing demands for speed, efficiency, and accuracy. This is where **test automation** comes in.

Definition of Test Automation

Test automation is the process of using specialized software tools to execute pre-scripted test cases on an application automatically. Instead of manually clicking through an interface or entering data, automation tools simulate user actions and verify expected outcomes.

Why Test Automation is Important

Automating tests can significantly improve the efficiency and effectiveness of the software testing process. Some key benefits include:

- **Speed** – Automated tests execute much faster than manual tests.
- **Reusability** – Test scripts can be reused across different test cycles and projects.
- **Accuracy** – Reduces human errors that occur in manual testing.
- **Coverage** – Allows for comprehensive testing, including large-scale regression testing.
- **Continuous Integration** – Integrates with CI/CD pipelines for automated testing in software development workflows.

When to Automate Tests

Not all test cases should be automated. You should focus automation efforts on:

1. **Repetitive Tasks** – Tests that need to be executed frequently, such as regression tests.
2. **High-Risk Areas** – Critical functionality where failure would have severe consequences.
3. **Performance and Load Testing** – Simulating thousands of users is impractical manually.
4. **Cross-Platform Testing** – Ensuring compatibility across multiple devices and browsers.

When NOT to Automate Tests

Automation is not always the best approach. Avoid automating:

- **Exploratory Testing** – Requires human intuition, creativity, and real-time decision-making.
- **One-Time Tests** – Tests that will not be executed frequently.
- **Frequent UI Changes** – Tests that need constant maintenance due to UI updates.

Common Test Automation Tools

There are various tools available for test automation, including:

- **Selenium** – Web application automation.
- **Cypress** – Modern JavaScript-based test automation for web apps.
- **Appium** – Mobile application testing for iOS and Android.
- **JUnit & TestNG** – Unit testing frameworks for Java-based applications.
- **Postman** – API testing automation.

By understanding test automation, you can decide when and how to use it effectively in your QA process. In the next section, you'll explore the benefits and challenges of automation and how to balance them for optimal software quality.

7.2. Benefits and Challenges of Automation

As you transition from manual to automated testing, it's essential to understand both the advantages and limitations of test automation. While automation enhances efficiency and accuracy, it also comes with challenges that require careful planning.

Benefits of Test Automation

1. Faster Test Execution

- Automated tests run significantly faster than manual tests.
- Reduces overall testing time, especially for large applications.

2. Increased Test Coverage

- Allows you to run thousands of test cases across different environments.
- Enables broader coverage of functionalities, including edge cases.

3. Improved Accuracy and Consistency

- Eliminates human errors that occur in manual testing.
- Ensures that test steps and validations are executed exactly the same way every time.

4. Cost Efficiency Over Time

- Although automation has an initial setup cost, it saves money in the long run.
- Reduces the number of testers needed for repetitive tasks.

5. Supports Continuous Integration and Delivery (CI/CD)

- Integrates with CI/CD pipelines for automated regression testing.
- Enables faster release cycles with confidence in software stability.

6. Reusability of Test Scripts

- Once written, test scripts can be reused across multiple projects and test cycles.
- Modular scripts allow easy updates and maintenance.

7. Enables Performance and Load Testing

- Simulates thousands of users interacting with the application.
- Helps identify bottlenecks and performance issues under stress.

Challenges of Test Automation

1. High Initial Investment

- Requires time and resources to set up automation frameworks and test scripts.
- Needs skilled professionals to write and maintain test scripts.

2. Frequent Maintenance of Test Scripts

- Automated tests may break due to UI and functionality changes.
- Requires ongoing script maintenance to ensure reliability.

3. Not Suitable for All Types of Testing

- Exploratory, usability, and ad-hoc testing require human intuition.
- Some tests may be too complex or expensive to automate effectively.

4. False Positives and False Negatives

- Automated tests may fail due to minor UI changes, even if the functionality works.
- Requires manual verification to confirm actual bugs.

5. Learning Curve and Tool Selection

- Testers need to learn scripting languages and automation tools.
- Choosing the right tool for your application can be challenging.

6. Infrastructure and Environment Dependencies

- Requires stable environments to ensure consistent test execution.
- External dependencies (e.g., databases, APIs) can cause test failures.

Key Takeaway

Test automation offers speed, accuracy, and efficiency but comes with challenges like maintenance and initial investment. To maximize the benefits, automate repetitive, high-risk, and regression test cases while keeping manual testing for exploratory and usability testing.

In the next section, you'll learn **when to automate and when not to** for an optimal testing strategy.

7.3. When to Automate and When Not To

Not every test case should be automated. Understanding when to automate and when to rely on manual testing is crucial for maintaining efficiency, accuracy, and cost-effectiveness in your testing process.

When to Automate Testing

Automation is best suited for tests that are repetitive, high-volume, or require precision. You should automate when:

1. Performing Regression Testing

- Automate test cases that need to be executed repeatedly after each code change.
- Helps catch defects introduced by new updates without manual effort.

2. Running Repetitive and Time-Consuming Tests

- Automate test cases that must be executed frequently across multiple builds or environments.
- Saves time by running tests overnight or in parallel.

3. Conducting Load, Performance, and Stress Testing

- Automation is essential for simulating thousands of users interacting with the application.
- Identifies performance bottlenecks that would be impossible to test manually.

4. Testing Large Data Sets

- Automated tests can handle large-scale data-driven testing efficiently.
- Ensures accuracy when validating data across different conditions.

5. Validating Critical Business Functions

- Automate test cases that check core application functionalities.
- Ensures that key business processes always work as expected.

6. Executing Cross-Browser and Cross-Platform Tests

- Automation helps test applications across multiple browsers (Chrome, Firefox, Edge) and devices (Windows, macOS, mobile).
- Reduces the effort required for manual cross-compatibility testing.

7. Supporting Continuous Integration/Continuous Deployment (CI/CD)

- Automated tests should be part of the CI/CD pipeline to detect issues early in development.
- Helps ensure stable releases with minimal manual intervention.

When NOT to Automate Testing

Some tests require human judgment, creativity, or are too costly to automate. Avoid automation in the following cases:

1. Exploratory Testing

- Automation cannot replace human intuition and creativity in finding unexpected bugs.

- Testers need to manually explore the application to uncover issues.

2. Usability and UI/UX Testing

- Automated tests cannot evaluate user experience, design, or intuitive navigation.
- Manual testers must assess how real users interact with the system.

3. Short-Term or One-Time Test Cases

- If a test case is only needed once or for a temporary feature, automating it is a waste of resources.
- Focus on manual execution for one-off validations.

4. Tests with Frequently Changing UI

- Automating UI tests for applications under rapid development leads to frequent script maintenance.
- Wait for UI stabilization before investing in automation.

5. Tests Requiring Physical Device Interactions

- Some scenarios, such as multi-touch gestures or hardware failures, are difficult to automate.
- Manual testing is better suited for these cases.

6. Low ROI Test Cases

- If the cost of automating a test outweighs its benefits, it's not worth automating.
- Prioritize automation for high-value test cases that provide long-term savings.

Key Takeaway

Automation should be used strategically. Focus on automating repetitive, stable, and high-impact test cases while keeping manual testing for exploratory, usability, and frequently changing test scenarios. By striking the right balance, you ensure an efficient and cost-effective QA process.

In the next chapter, you'll start learning **how to write automation scripts and get hands-on experience with automated testing tools.**

8. Writing Automation Scripts

8.1. Basics of Programming for Testers (Python, Java, JavaScript)

To become an effective automation tester, you need a basic understanding of programming. While you don't need to be a software developer, having a solid grasp of coding fundamentals will help you write test scripts, debug automation issues, and create maintainable test frameworks.

1. Why Programming is Important for Testers

- **Automation scripts are written in code** – Understanding programming languages allows you to create, modify, and debug test cases.
- **Scripting enhances test efficiency** – Writing scripts lets you automate repetitive tasks, reducing manual effort.
- **Debugging and troubleshooting skills are essential** – When a test fails, knowing how to read and fix the script is crucial.
- **Most test automation frameworks require coding** – Selenium, Cypress, and Appium rely on languages like Python, Java, and JavaScript.

2. Choosing a Programming Language for Test Automation

Different automation tools support different languages. The three most popular choices for automation testing are **Python, Java, and JavaScript.**

Python for Test Automation

Python is widely used for automation due to its simplicity and readability.

Advantages:

- Easy-to-learn syntax, ideal for beginners.
- Strong support for automation frameworks (Selenium, PyTest, Robot Framework).

- Rich set of libraries for testing, data handling, and web automation.

Basic Python Concepts for Testers:

- Variables and data types (int, float, string, list, dictionary)
- Conditional statements (if-else)
- Loops (for, while)
- Functions and modules
- File handling (reading/writing test data)
- Exception handling (try-except)

Example: Simple Python Script to Open a Website with Selenium

```
from selenium import webdriver

driver = webdriver.Chrome()  # Initialize Chrome browser

driver.get("https://www.google.com")  # Open Google

print(driver.title)  # Print page title

driver.quit()  # Close browser
```

Java for Test Automation

Java is a powerful and widely used language in enterprise automation testing.

Advantages:

- Strongly typed and object-oriented, making code more structured.
- Preferred for Selenium WebDriver automation.
- Robust support for test frameworks like TestNG and JUnit.

Basic Java Concepts for Testers:

- Data types (`int, double, String, boolean`)
- Control flow (`if-else, loops`)

- Methods and classes
- Object-Oriented Programming (OOP) principles (encapsulation, inheritance, polymorphism)
- Exception handling (try-catch)

Example: Simple Java Script to Open a Website with Selenium

```
import org.openqa.selenium.WebDriver;

import org.openqa.selenium.chrome.ChromeDriver;

public class OpenGoogle {

    public static void main(String[] args) {

        WebDriver driver = new ChromeDriver(); // Initialize Chrome
browser

        driver.get("https://www.google.com"); // Open Google

        System.out.println(driver.getTitle()); // Print page title

        driver.quit(); // Close browser

    }

}
```

JavaScript for Test Automation

JavaScript is a key language for web-based automation, especially with frameworks like Cypress and Playwright.

Advantages:

- Best for front-end testing and browser automation.
- Used in modern test automation frameworks like Cypress and WebDriverIO.
- Works well with CI/CD pipelines for fast, scalable testing.

Basic JavaScript Concepts for Testers:

- Variables (`let, const, var`)
- Functions and callbacks
- Loops and conditional statements
- Working with the DOM (useful for UI automation)
- Promises and async/await (handling asynchronous test execution)

Example: Simple JavaScript Script to Open a Website with Cypress

```
describe('Google Test', () => {

    it('Opens Google and verifies title', () => {

        cy.visit('https://www.google.com'); // Open Google

        cy.title().should('include', 'Google'); // Verify title
contains "Google"

    });

});
```

3. Best Practices for Learning Programming as a Tester

- **Start with the basics** – Learn fundamental concepts before diving into frameworks.
- **Write small automation scripts** – Practice simple scripts to automate basic tasks.
- **Follow online tutorials and courses** – Platforms like Coursera, Udemy, and freeCodeCamp offer beginner-friendly programming courses.
- **Join coding communities** – Engage in communities like Stack Overflow, GitHub, and automation testing forums.
- **Work on real automation projects** – Apply your skills to real-world automation tasks and gradually increase complexity.
- **Understand debugging techniques** – Learn to read error messages

and fix script failures effectively.

Key Takeaway

Mastering a programming language is essential for automation testers. Python is best for beginners due to its simplicity, Java is great for structured enterprise automation, and JavaScript is ideal for web-based testing. Choose a language based on your project needs and testing goals.

In the next section, you'll learn **how to write your first automation script and execute automated test cases effectively.**

8.2. Writing Your First Automation Script

Writing your first automation script is a crucial step in your journey toward test automation. This section will guide you through setting up a basic automation script using **Selenium WebDriver**, a popular automation tool for web testing.

1. Setting Up Your Automation Environment

Before writing your first script, you need to set up your test automation environment. You can search YouTube for tutorials on how to install all the software mentioned in this section. Additionally, I provide a few links below to guide you.

Step 1: Install Required Software

Install Python (if using Python) or **Java** (if using Java).

Learn how to install Python here https://www.datacamp.com/blog/how-to-install-python or here https://www.youtube.com/watch?v=YKSpANU8jPE.

Learn how to install Java here https://www.youtube.com/watch?v=PQk9O03cukQ or here https://www.youtube.com/watch?v=SQykK40fFds.

Install a code editor or IDE:

- **PyCharm** (for Python)
- **Eclipse** or **IntelliJ IDEA** (for Java)
- **VS Code** (for JavaScript, Python, or Java)

Learn how to install Pycharm here: https://www.youtube.com/watch?v=Tmu_fkFwlvw.

Download and install Selenium WebDriver:

- Python: Install using `pip install selenium`
- Java: Download Selenium JAR files or use Maven dependencies
- JavaScript: Install using `npm install selenium-webdriver`

Learn how to install Selenium WebDriver here https://www.youtube.com/watch?v=OuhbUUVtDzs or here https://www.youtube.com/watch?v=gVXcVcTRXd0.

Step 2: Install a Web Browser and WebDriver

- **Google Chrome** → Install **ChromeDriver**
- **Mozilla Firefox** → Install **GeckoDriver**
- **Microsoft Edge** → Install **EdgeDriver**

Learn how to install and configure ChromeDriver here: https://www.youtube.com/watch?v=4gJAAeEPxFo.

2. Writing Your First Selenium Automation Script

Example: Automating a Website Login (Python, Java, JavaScript)

Python: Selenium Automation Script

This Python script opens a website, enters login credentials, and clicks the login button.

```python
from selenium import webdriver
from selenium.webdriver.common.by import By
from selenium.webdriver.common.keys import Keys

# Initialize the Chrome WebDriver
driver = webdriver.Chrome()

# Open the website
driver.get("https://example.com/login")

# Find the username and password fields and enter credentials
driver.find_element(By.ID, "username").send_keys("testuser")
driver.find_element(By.ID, "password").send_keys("password123")

# Click the login button
driver.find_element(By.ID, "loginButton").click()

# Verify login success by checking the page title
print("Login Successful:", driver.title)

# Close the browser
driver.quit()
```

Java: Selenium Automation Script

```
import org.openqa.selenium.By;

import org.openqa.selenium.WebDriver;

import org.openqa.selenium.WebElement;

import org.openqa.selenium.chrome.ChromeDriver;


public class LoginTest {

    public static void main(String[] args) {

        // Set up WebDriver

        WebDriver driver = new ChromeDriver();


        // Open the website

        driver.get("https://example.com/login");


        // Locate username and password fields and enter credentials

        driver.findElement(By.id("username")).sendKeys("testuser");

driver.findElement(By.id("password")).sendKeys("password123");


        // Click login button

        driver.findElement(By.id("loginButton")).click();


        // Verify login success

        System.out.println("Login Successful: " + driver.getTitle());
```

```
        // Close the browser
        driver.quit();
    }
}
```

JavaScript: Selenium WebDriver Automation Script

```
const { Builder, By } = require('selenium-webdriver');

(async function loginTest() {
    let driver = await new Builder().forBrowser('chrome').build();

    try {
        // Open the website
        await driver.get('https://example.com/login');

        // Locate username and password fields and enter
credentials
        await
driver.findElement(By.id('username')).sendKeys('testuser');
        await
driver.findElement(By.id('password')).sendKeys('password123');

        // Click the login button
        await driver.findElement(By.id('loginButton')).click();
```

```
        // Verify login success
        let title = await driver.getTitle();
        console.log("Login Successful: " + title);
    } finally {
        // Close the browser
        await driver.quit();
    }
})();
```

3. Running Your Automation Script

Python

- Save your script as test_login.py.
- Open the command line and navigate to the script's directory.
- Run: `python test_login.py`

Java

- Save your script as `LoginTest.java`.
- Compile and run it using:

```
javac LoginTest.java
java LoginTest
```

JavaScript

- Save your script as `test_login.js`.
- Run using Node.js: `node test_login.js`

4. Best Practices for Writing Automation Scripts

1. Use clear and descriptive element locators

- Prefer `By.ID` or `By.NAME` instead of `By.XPATH` for stability.

2. Add assertions to verify expected outcomes

- Use assertions (`assert` in Python, `Assert.assertEquals` in Java) to validate expected results.

3. Avoid hardcoding test data

- Use external data sources (CSV, JSON, databases) to make tests reusable.

4. Implement wait conditions

- Use explicit waits (`WebDriverWait`) to handle dynamic page elements.

5. Organize code into functions

- Encapsulate reusable steps in functions or methods for better maintainability.

6. Use logging for debugging

- Print messages or use logging frameworks (`log4j` for Java, `logging` module for Python).

7. Run tests in headless mode when needed

- For faster execution in CI/CD pipelines, enable **headless mode** (`options.headless = True`).

Key Takeaway

You have successfully written and executed your first automation script! Understanding the basics of programming and automation tools is essential for building robust test scripts. In the next section, you'll learn how to **enhance automation scripts with assertions, data-driven testing, and reporting features.**

8.3. Debugging and Troubleshooting Automation Scripts

Automation scripts often fail due to various reasons such as incorrect element locators, timing issues, or unexpected changes in the application under test. In this section, you'll learn how to effectively **debug and troubleshoot** your automation scripts to ensure smooth execution.

1. Common Reasons for Automation Script Failures

1.1. Incorrect Element Locators

- Using outdated or incorrect **XPath, CSS selectors, or IDs** can cause failures.
- The web page structure may have changed, making the locator invalid.

Solution:

Use stable locators like **ID** or **Name** instead of dynamic XPaths.

- Verify locators using browser **DevTools (F12 → Inspect Element)**.
- Use `findElements()` to check if an element exists before interacting with it.

1.2. Timing Issues (Synchronization Errors)

- If your script tries to interact with an element **before it appears**, it will fail.
- Some elements take time to load due to AJAX requests or animations.

Solution:

Implement **Explicit Waits** instead of static `sleep()`.

```
from selenium.webdriver.support.ui import WebDriverWait

from selenium.webdriver.support import expected_conditions as EC

wait = WebDriverWait(driver, 10)

element = wait.until(EC.visibility_of_element_located((By.ID,
"loginButton")))
```

Use **Implicit Waits** to wait for elements throughout the script.

```
driver.manage().timeouts().implicitlyWait(10, TimeUnit.SECONDS);
```

1.3. Stale Element Exception

- Happens when the element is refreshed or reloaded before interaction.

Solution:

- Re-locate the element before interacting with it.
- Use **Explicit Waits** to handle dynamic elements.

1.4. Browser Compatibility Issues

- The script may work in **Chrome** but fail in **Firefox** or **Edge**.

Solution:

- Run cross-browser tests using different **WebDriver versions**.
- Use cloud testing services like **Sauce Labs, BrowserStack** for compatibility testing.

1.5. Hardcoded Test Data

- Hardcoding values like **username/password** can make scripts unreliable.

Solution:

- Use **external data sources** (CSV, Excel, JSON, Databases).
- Implement **parameterization** in your test framework.

2. Debugging Techniques for Automation Scripts

2.1. Enable Logging and Debugging Mode

- Python (Logging Module)

```
import logging

logging.basicConfig(level=logging.DEBUG)

logging.debug("Debug message")
```

- Java (Log4j Example)

```
import org.apache.logging.log4j.Logger;

private static final Logger log =
LogManager.getLogger(YourClass.class);

log.debug("Debugging message");
```

- JavaScript (Console Logs)

```
console.log("Debugging message");
```

2.2. Take Screenshots on Failure

- Capture screenshots when a test fails to analyze the issue.

- Python (Selenium Example)

```
driver.save_screenshot("error_screenshot.png")
```

- Java (Selenium Example)

```
File screenshot = ((TakesScreenshot)
driver).getScreenshotAs(OutputType.FILE);

FileUtils.copyFile(screenshot, new File("error.png"));
```

2.3. Use Debugging Tools

- **Python**: Use `pdb` for step-by-step debugging.

```
import pdb; pdb.set_trace()
```

- **Java**: Use breakpoints in **IntelliJ IDEA** or **Eclipse Debugger**.
- **JavaScript**: Use debugger; inside your script for browser debugging.

2.4. Print Stack Traces for Error Analysis

- **Python:**

```
import traceback

try:

    driver.find_element(By.ID, "login").click()

except Exception as e:

    print(traceback.format_exc())
```

- Java

```
try {
    driver.findElement(By.id("login")).click();
} catch (Exception e) {
    e.printStackTrace();
}
```

3. Troubleshooting Automation Script Failures

3.1. Handling Pop-ups and Alerts

- **Accept or dismiss browser alerts**

```
alert = driver.switch_to.alert
alert.accept()  # or alert.dismiss()
```

- Handle authentication pop-ups

```
driver.get("https://username:password@example.com")
```

3.2. Dealing with Dynamic Elements

- If elements change frequently, use **dynamic XPath** with partial attributes.

```
driver.find_element(By.XPATH,
"//button[contains(text(),'Login')]").click()
```

3.3. Verifying Network Requests and Console Logs

- Use **Browser DevTools (F12 → Network Tab)** to check API responses.
- Capture browser logs in Selenium.

```
LogEntries logs = driver.manage().logs().get(LogType.BROWSER);
for (LogEntry log : logs) {
    System.out.println(log.getMessage());
}
```

3.4. Handling Page Load Errors

- Check if the page loaded successfully before performing actions.

```
assert "Dashboard" in driver.title, "Page did not load properly"
```

4. Best Practices for Debugging Automation Scripts

1. Write modular test scripts

- Use functions/methods to separate reusable code.

2. Log detailed error messages

- Print messages at each step to identify failure points.

3. Use soft assertions when needed

- Allows the test to continue even if one assertion fails.

4. Run tests in headless mode for faster debugging

- `options.headless = True` in Selenium WebDriver.

5. Use version control (Git) to track changes

- Helps identify when failures started occurring.

Key Takeaway

Debugging and troubleshooting automation scripts is a crucial skill for every QA tester. By using effective logging, error handling, and debugging tools, you can quickly resolve issues and make your test scripts **more reliable, stable, and efficient**.

8.4. Practice Exercises on writing, debugging, and optimizing automation scripts

To reinforce your learning, complete the following five exercises. These exercises range from simple to very difficult, testing your ability to write, debug, and optimize automation scripts. Solutions are provided at the end of the chapter.

Exercise 1: Automating a Simple Google Search

Task:

Write a Selenium script to:

1. Open the Google homepage (https://www.google.com).
2. Enter "Selenium WebDriver" into the search box.
3. Click the Google Search button.
4. Print the title of the search results page.

Exercise 2: Verifying a Login Functionality

Task:

Write a Selenium script to:

1. Open the login page of any demo website (e.g., `https://practicetestautomation.com/practice-test-login/`).
2. Enter the username: "`student`".
3. Enter the password: "`Password123`".
4. Click the Login button.
5. Verify that the login is successful by checking if the "Logged In Successfully" message appears.

Exercise 3: Handling a Dynamic Drop-Down Menu

Task:

Write a Selenium script to:

1. Open https://www.selenium.dev/selenium/web/dynamic.html.
2. Click a **drop-down menu** that loads dynamically.
3. Select the option "Option 3" from the list.
4. Verify that the selected option is "Option 3".

Exercise 4: Scraping Multiple Elements from a Web Page

Task:

Write a Selenium script to:

1. Open https://news.ycombinator.com/.
2. Extract and print the **top 5 news headlines** along with their URLs.
3. Store the extracted data in a **CSV file**.

Exercise 5: Automating an End-to-End E-Commerce Checkout

Task:

Write a Selenium script to:

1. Open https://www.saucedemo.com/.

2. Login using the credentials:

- Username: `standard_user`
- Password: `secret_sauce`

3. Add the first two products to the cart.

4. Proceed to checkout and enter:

- First Name: `John`
- Last Name: `Doe`
- ZIP Code: `12345`

5. Complete the purchase and verify that the "Thank you for your order" message appears.

8.5. Solutions to Practice Exercises

Solution 1: Automating a Simple Google Search

```
from selenium import webdriver

from selenium.webdriver.common.by import By

from selenium.webdriver.common.keys import Keys


# Initialize WebDriver

driver = webdriver.Chrome()
```

```
# Open Google
driver.get("https://www.google.com")

# Locate search box, enter query, and press ENTER
search_box = driver.find_element(By.NAME, "q")
search_box.send_keys("Selenium WebDriver" + Keys.RETURN)

# Print page title
print("Page Title:", driver.title)

# Close browser
driver.quit()
```

Solution 2: Verifying a Login Functionality

```
from selenium import webdriver
from selenium.webdriver.common.by import By

# Initialize WebDriver
driver = webdriver.Chrome()

# Open login page
driver.get("https://practicetestautomation.com/practice-test-login/")
```

```
# Enter username and password
driver.find_element(By.ID, "username").send_keys("student")
driver.find_element(By.ID, "password").send_keys("Password123")

# Click login button
driver.find_element(By.ID, "submit").click()

# Verify login success
success_message = driver.find_element(By.TAG_NAME, "h1").text
assert "Logged In Successfully" in success_message

print("Login Test Passed")

# Close browser
driver.quit()
```

Solution 3: Handling a Dynamic Drop-Down Menu

```
from selenium import webdriver
from selenium.webdriver.common.by import By
from selenium.webdriver.support.ui import WebDriverWait
from selenium.webdriver.support import expected_conditions as EC
```

```
# Initialize WebDriver
driver = webdriver.Chrome()


# Open test page
driver.get("https://www.selenium.dev/selenium/web/dynamic.html")


# Wait for drop-down to be clickable and click it
dropdown = WebDriverWait(driver, 10).until(
    EC.element_to_be_clickable((By.ID, "dynamicDropdown"))
)
dropdown.click()


# Select 'Option 3'
option = WebDriverWait(driver, 10).until(
    EC.element_to_be_clickable((By.XPATH, "//option[text()='Option 3']"))
)
option.click()


# Verify selection
assert option.text == "Option 3"


print("Dropdown Test Passed")
```

```
# Close browser

driver.quit()
```

Solution 4: Scraping Multiple Elements from a Web Page

```
import csv

from selenium import webdriver

from selenium.webdriver.common.by import By


# Initialize WebDriver

driver = webdriver.Chrome()


# Open news page

driver.get("https://news.ycombinator.com/")


# Extract top 5 headlines

headlines = driver.find_elements(By.CLASS_NAME, "titleline")[:5]


# Store results in CSV

with open("headlines.csv", "w", newline="", encoding="utf-8") as file:

    writer = csv.writer(file)

    writer.writerow(["Headline", "URL"])


    for headline in headlines:
```

```
        link = headline.find_element(By.TAG_NAME, "a")
        writer.writerow([link.text, link.get_attribute("href")])


print("Scraping Completed - Results Saved in headlines.csv")


# Close browser
driver.quit()
```

Solution 5: Automating an End-to-End E-Commerce Checkout

```
from selenium import webdriver
from selenium.webdriver.common.by import By
from selenium.webdriver.common.keys import Keys
import time


# Initialize WebDriver
driver = webdriver.Chrome()


# Open e-commerce site
driver.get("https://www.saucedemo.com/")


# Login
driver.find_element(By.ID, "user-name").send_keys("standard_user")
driver.find_element(By.ID, "password").send_keys("secret_sauce")
```

```
driver.find_element(By.ID, "login-button").click()


# Add first two items to cart

driver.find_elements(By.CLASS_NAME, "btn_inventory")[0].click()

driver.find_elements(By.CLASS_NAME, "btn_inventory")[1].click()


# Go to cart

driver.find_element(By.CLASS_NAME, "shopping_cart_link").click()


# Proceed to checkout

driver.find_element(By.ID, "checkout").click()


# Enter checkout details

driver.find_element(By.ID, "first-name").send_keys("John")

driver.find_element(By.ID, "last-name").send_keys("Doe")

driver.find_element(By.ID, "postal-code").send_keys("12345")

driver.find_element(By.ID, "continue").click()


# Complete purchase

driver.find_element(By.ID, "finish").click()


# Verify successful order

confirmation_text = driver.find_element(By.CLASS_NAME, "complete-
header").text
```

```
assert "Thank you for your order" in confirmation_text


print("E-Commerce Checkout Test Passed")


# Close browser
driver.quit()
```

Key Takeaway

These exercises help you build a strong foundation in automation testing. By solving them, you improve your ability to:

- Interact with web elements.
- Handle dynamic elements and waits.
- Debug script failures.
- Automate real-world testing scenarios.

Now, proceed to the next chapter where we dive deeper into **advanced automation techniques**.

9. How to Get Your First QA Job

9.1. Writing a Strong QA Resume

A well-crafted resume is essential to stand out in the competitive field of QA testing. Your resume should highlight your skills, experience, and ability to contribute effectively as a QA tester.

1. Key Components of a Strong QA Resume

Ensure your resume includes the following essential sections:

Contact Information: Name, phone number, email, LinkedIn profile, and portfolio (if applicable).

Professional Summary: A brief 2-3 sentence summary of your QA skills and experience.

Technical Skills: List relevant QA skills, including:

- Manual and automated testing
- Test case design
- Bug tracking tools (Jira, Bugzilla, etc.)
- Test automation tools (Selenium, Cypress, etc.)
- Programming languages (Python, Java, JavaScript, etc.)

Work Experience (if applicable):

- List job title, company name, and employment dates.
- Highlight QA responsibilities and accomplishments in bullet points.
- Use metrics where possible (e.g., "Reduced bug occurrence by 30% through effective test case management").

Projects and Hands-on Experience (for entry-level testers):

- Include personal, freelance, or open-source testing projects.
- Provide links to GitHub repositories, test plans, or bug reports.

Certifications and Education:

- List degrees, diplomas, or certifications (e.g., ISTQB, Certified Selenium Tester).

Soft Skills (Optional but recommended):

- Communication, analytical thinking, problem-solving, teamwork, and attention to detail.

2. Resume Formatting Best Practices

- **Keep it concise**: Aim for a one-page resume (two pages if you have extensive experience).
- **Use a professional font**: Stick to readable fonts like Arial, Calibri, or Times New Roman (size 10-12).
- **Use bullet points**: Clearly outline responsibilities and accomplishments for easy readability.
- **Avoid unnecessary details**: Focus on relevant QA-related experience and skills.
- **Proofread for errors**: Spelling and grammar mistakes can create a bad impression.

3. Tailoring Your Resume for Each Job Application

- **Match keywords**: Use the same terminology found in the job description.
- **Highlight relevant skills**: If the job focuses on automation, emphasize your experience with automation tools.
- **Customize your summary**: Tailor your professional summary to align with the role.
- **Emphasize transferable skills**: If you are transitioning from another career, highlight skills relevant to QA (e.g., analytical thinking, documentation, or troubleshooting).

4. Common Mistakes to Avoid

- **Using generic resumes for all job applications**: Always customize your resume.

- **Listing outdated or irrelevant skills**: Focus on modern QA tools and practices.
- **Ignoring soft skills**: QA roles often require communication and teamwork.
- **Neglecting to include personal projects**: If you're a beginner, showcase real testing experience through projects.

Key Takeaway

Your resume is your first opportunity to make a strong impression on recruiters and hiring managers. A well-structured, keyword-optimized, and tailored resume can significantly increase your chances of landing your first QA job.

9.2. Preparing for QA Interviews (Common Interview Questions)

A strong interview performance is crucial to securing your first QA job. You need to demonstrate your technical skills, problem-solving ability, and understanding of software testing principles.

1. Types of QA Interview Questions

QA interviews typically include:

- **General Questions** – Assess your background, motivation, and understanding of QA.
- **Technical Questions** – Test your knowledge of software testing concepts, methodologies, and tools.
- **Behavioral Questions** – Evaluate how you handle real-world testing scenarios and teamwork.
- **Practical Assignments** – Require you to analyze test cases, find defects, or write test scripts.

2. Common QA Interview Questions and How to Answer Them

A. General QA Questions:

i. Tell me about yourself.

- Keep it concise. Highlight your background, QA skills, and relevant experience.
- Example: *"I have a background in computer science with hands-on experience in manual and automated testing. I've worked on test case design, bug reporting, and automation using Selenium."*

ii. Why do you want to work as a QA tester?

- Emphasize problem-solving, attention to detail, and passion for quality.
- Example: *"I enjoy ensuring software functions as expected and improving user experience. QA allows me to apply my analytical skills to identify and resolve defects."*

iii. What are the differences between QA, QC, and Testing?

- **QA (Quality Assurance)** – Focuses on preventing defects through processes.
- **QC (Quality Control)** – Involves inspecting and validating products to meet quality standards.
- **Testing** – The process of executing software to find bugs.

B. Technical QA Questions

i. What are the different types of software testing?

- **Functional Testing** – Ensures the software meets requirements (e.g., unit testing, integration testing).
- **Non-Functional Testing** – Tests aspects like performance, security, and usability.

ii. Explain the Software Testing Life Cycle (STLC).

- **Requirement Analysis → Test Planning → Test Case Design → Test Execution → Defect Reporting → Test Closure**

iii. What is the difference between smoke testing and sanity testing?

- **Smoke Testing** – A high-level check to confirm the application's stability.
- **Sanity Testing** – A narrow, focused check after bug fixes to ensure specific functionality works.

iv. What is boundary value analysis (BVA)?

- A technique to test edge cases by checking values at the boundary (e.g., testing input fields with 0, 1, and max limits).

v. What is equivalence partitioning?

- A technique that divides input data into valid and invalid groups to reduce the number of test cases.

vi. What is a test case? What should a good test case include?

- A test case is a set of conditions to verify software behavior. It should include: *Test Case ID, Description, Preconditions, Steps to Execute, Expected Result, Actual Result, Status (Pass/Fail)*

vii. What tools have you used for bug tracking?

- Mention tools like **Jira, Bugzilla, Mantis, or Redmine** and briefly describe how you used them.

C. Behavioral Questions

i. Describe a time when you found a critical bug. How did you handle it?

- Follow the **STAR (Situation, Task, Action, Result)** method.
- Example: *"I was testing a payment system and found that credit card transactions were failing. I documented the issue with logs and screenshots, reported it in Jira, and worked with developers to resolve it before release."*

ii. How do you handle conflicts with developers?

- Emphasize communication and teamwork.

- Example: *"I focus on facts and evidence, explaining issues clearly with supporting data. If needed, I involve the team lead to find a resolution."*

iii. What do you do when you disagree with a test plan or requirement?

- Explain how you provide constructive feedback and suggest improvements.

D. Practical Assignments (Hands-on QA Tasks)

Employers may ask you to:

- Write test cases for a login page.
- Identify bugs in a given application.
- Execute a sample test scenario.
- Write a basic automation script in Selenium or another tool.

Prepare for these by practicing **real-world testing scenarios** and **automation scripts**.

3. Tips for Succeeding in Your QA Interview

- **Study the job description** – Align your answers with the required skills.
- **Practice mock interviews** – Answer questions aloud to build confidence.
- **Review testing tools** – Be familiar with industry-standard tools (Jira, Selenium, etc.).
- **Be prepared for hands-on tasks** – Brush up on test case writing and basic automation.
- **Stay professional and confident** – Speak clearly, show enthusiasm, and demonstrate your problem-solving skills.

Key Takeaway

QA interviews assess both your **technical expertise** and **problem-solving approach**. By preparing thoroughly, practicing real-world test scenarios, and confidently communicating your skills, you increase your chances of landing your first QA job.

9.3. Freelancing & Remote Work Opportunities in QA

Freelancing and remote work in QA provide flexible job opportunities that allow you to work with global clients and gain hands-on experience without being tied to a physical office. Whether you're looking to start your QA career or expand your expertise, freelancing and remote jobs can be a great option.

1. Benefits of Freelancing & Remote QA Work

- **Flexibility** – Choose your own schedule and work from anywhere.
- **Diverse Experience** – Work with various companies, industries, and technologies.
- **Income Potential** – Earn based on your expertise, project scope, and client demand.
- **Skill Growth** – Gain exposure to different testing methodologies, tools, and real-world scenarios.
- **Build a Portfolio** – Strengthen your resume with real-world testing projects.

2. Where to Find Freelance & Remote QA Jobs

A. Freelance Platforms (Search their names on Google)

1. **Upwork** – Offers both short-term and long-term QA projects.
2. **Fiverr** – Create a profile and offer QA testing services.
3. **Freelancer** – Browse QA testing gigs and submit proposals.
4. **Toptal** – Connects top freelancers with high-paying clients (requires passing a screening process).
5. **PeoplePerHour** – A good platform for offering specialized QA services.

B. Remote Job Boards (Search their names on Google)

1. **We Work Remotely** – Lists high-quality remote QA jobs.
2. **Remote OK** – Features job postings from global tech companies.

3. **FlexJobs** – Specializes in remote, part-time, and freelance work.
4. **AngelList** – Find remote QA jobs at tech startups.
5. **Turing** – Matches QA testers with long-term remote positions. Learn more here: https://www.turing.com/jobs/remote-software-testing-engineer.

C. Crowdsourced Testing Platforms (Search their names on Google)

1. **uTest** – Get paid to test apps and websites for real-world bugs.
2. **Test IO** – Participate in usability and exploratory testing projects.
3. **UserTesting** – Conduct usability tests and provide feedback.
4. **Bugcrowd** – If you're interested in security testing, this platform offers bug bounty programs.

3. Skills You Need for Freelance & Remote QA Work

To stand out in the competitive freelancing market, you must develop essential QA skills:

- **Manual Testing** – Ability to test web, mobile, and desktop applications thoroughly.
- **Automation Testing** – Proficiency in Selenium, Cypress, or Playwright can increase job opportunities.
- **Bug Reporting** – Familiarity with bug tracking tools like Jira, Bugzilla, and Trello.
- **API Testing** – Knowledge of Postman, RestAssured, or SoapUI is an advantage.
- **Performance Testing** – Experience with JMeter or LoadRunner is useful for certain projects.
- **Good Communication** – Strong written and verbal skills for reporting bugs and interacting with clients.

4. How to Get Started with Freelancing & Remote QA Jobs

Step 1: Build Your Online Presence

- **Create a professional profile** on platforms like Upwork, Fiverr, and LinkedIn.

- **Showcase your expertise** – Highlight your QA skills, certifications, and tools you use.
- **Develop a portfolio** – Include sample test cases, bug reports, and automation scripts.

Step 2: Apply for Entry-Level Freelance Projects

- Start with **small projects** to build credibility.
- Apply to **crowdsourced testing platforms** for hands-on experience.
- Offer competitive rates initially, then increase as you gain experience.

Step 3: Network & Join QA Communities (Search their names on Google)

- Engage in **QA forums** like **TestGuild**, **Ministry of Testing**, and **Reddit's r/QualityAssurance**.
- Participate in **LinkedIn QA groups** to connect with recruiters and potential clients.
- Attend **webinars and online meetups** to stay updated on industry trends.

Step 4: Keep Learning & Upskilling

- Take online courses on Udemy, Coursera, or Test Automation University.
- Stay updated on **emerging QA tools** and technologies.
- Get certified in **ISTQB, Selenium, or API testing** to boost your credibility.

Step 5: Deliver Quality Work & Get Positive Reviews

- Be thorough in testing and reporting bugs.
- Meet deadlines and communicate professionally with clients.
- Request testimonials from satisfied clients to improve your profile ranking.

5. Challenges of Freelancing & Remote QA Jobs (and How to Overcome Them)

Challenge	Solution
Finding first clients	Apply to small projects, network, and offer competitive pricing.
Managing multiple clients	Use project management tools like Trello or Asana.
Inconsistent income	Build long-term relationships with clients and diversify income streams.
Staying motivated	Set daily work schedules and maintain a work-life balance.
Keeping up with industry trends	Take courses, join QA communities, and practice new tools.

Key Takeaway

Freelancing and remote QA jobs can be a great way to start your testing career, gain experience, and earn income on your own terms. By building your skills, applying for relevant projects, and continuously improving, you can establish yourself as a successful QA freelancer or remote tester.

9.4. Unlocking Part 2: Advanced QA Automation—Mastering Test Frameworks, API Testing, and CI/CD Integration

Software testing has evolved significantly over the years, transitioning from simple manual checks to complex automated solutions that integrate seamlessly into modern development workflows. As the industry moves towards **continuous integration, rapid development cycles, and AI-driven testing**, QA professionals must **adapt, expand their knowledge, and refine their skills** to stay competitive.

In **Part 1**, you built a strong foundation in both manual and automated testing, mastering essential concepts such as writing test cases, using test management tools, executing manual and automated tests, and reporting bugs effectively. You also learned how to transition into automation testing by understanding basic scripting, debugging techniques, and best practices for writing test scripts.

Now, in **Part 2**, we take your QA expertise to the next level by diving deep into advanced automation techniques, API and performance testing, test framework development, CI/CD integration, security testing, mobile app testing, and career growth strategies. The goal of this part is to equip you with the skills and knowledge required to become a highly sought-after QA automation expert.

9.4.1. What You'll Learn in Part 2 of the Book

In this part, you'll go beyond **basic test automation** and explore **advanced techniques** that allow you to **build, scale, and optimize automation frameworks, ensure high-quality software releases, and integrate seamlessly into modern DevOps pipelines**.

Advanced Automation Techniques

- **Data-Driven and Keyword-Driven Testing** – Learn how to design reusable and scalable test scripts by separating test data from test logic.
- **Test Framework Development** – Build and maintain robust **automation frameworks** using tools like **Selenium, Cypress, Appium, and Playwright**.
- **CI/CD Integration** – Implement **automated testing** in **continuous integration and deployment (CI/CD) pipelines** using tools like

Jenkins, GitHub Actions, and GitLab CI.

- **Best Practices for Automation Maintenance** – Learn how to create **modular, reusable, and easy-to-maintain** automation scripts that stand the test of time.

Specialized Testing Domains

- **API Testing** – Understand how to test web APIs, write API test cases, and automate API testing using tools like **Postman and REST Assured**.
- **Performance Testing** – Explore tools like **JMeter and LoadRunner** to measure application speed, scalability, and responsiveness under load.
- **Security Testing** – Learn about **OWASP Top 10 vulnerabilities**, how to identify security flaws, and strategies for securing applications.
- **Mobile App Testing** – Gain hands-on experience in testing Android and iOS applications using **Appium, Espresso, and XCUITest.**

Quality Metrics & Reporting

- **Essential QA Metrics** – Learn how to measure and track software quality using industry-standard QA metrics.
- **Generating QA Reports** – Master the art of creating **professional test reports** for stakeholders, project managers, and developers.
- **Tracking and Improving Software Quality** – Learn best practices for continuous **monitoring, measuring, and improving** software quality in your organization.

Troubleshooting & Test Maintenance

- **Debugging & Troubleshooting** – Learn advanced techniques for **diagnosing and fixing test failures** in automation.

- **Handling Flaky Tests** – Discover strategies to **reduce test flakiness,** making your automated tests **more reliable and consistent.**
- **Long-Term Test Maintenance** – Develop strategies for managing and maintaining large-scale **automation suites** effectively.

Future-Proofing Your QA Career

- **AI-Powered Test Automation** – Stay ahead of the curve by exploring the impact of **AI and machine learning in test automation.**
- **Low-Code/No-Code Automation Tools** – Understand how tools like **TestProject, Katalon Studio, and Testim** are changing the automation landscape.
- **Emerging Trends in QA** – Gain insights into the **latest advancements** in **software testing, automation, and DevOps.**
- **Building a Personal Brand in QA** – Learn how to showcase your **manual and automation testing skills** through a **personal website, GitHub projects, and online portfolio.**

9.4.2. Be on the Lookout for Part 2!

The journey to becoming an expert in QA automation and software testing doesn't stop here. Part 2 of this book will serve as your definitive guide to mastering advanced QA topics, expanding your technical skills, and positioning yourself for high-paying roles in the industry.

This upcoming volume is designed to **push your skills beyond the basics,** helping you stand out in the competitive world of software testing. Whether you're an aspiring automation engineer, a seasoned tester looking to enhance your expertise, or a professional aiming for leadership roles, Part 2 will provide you with the advanced knowledge you need to thrive.

Stay tuned for the release of Part 2 on **Amazon and other major book retailers.** It's coming **soon,** packed with actionable insights, real-world examples, and expert strategies to help you master **advanced automation,**

API testing, CI/CD integration, and much more. Keep an eye out—you won't want to miss it!

9.5. How to Get Further Help & Support

If you find out you still need further help or support, or if you want to share your experience of QA testing with me, don't hesitate to use my support email address below to send your request. I'll get back to you in 12 hours or less. I promise.

Cheers,

Bolakale Aremu

AB Publisher LLC

ABPublisherLLC@gmail.com

10. References

Fewster, M., and Graham, D. 1999. *Software Test Automation: Effective Use of Test Execution Tools*. Addison-Wesley.

Kaner, C., Falk, J., and Nguyen, H. Q. 1999. *Testing Computer Software, 2nd Edition*. Wiley.

Myers, G. J., Sandler, C., and Badgett, T. 2011. *The Art of Software Testing, 3rd Edition*. Wiley.

Crispin, L., and Gregory, J. 2009. *Agile Testing: A Practical Guide for Testers and Agile Teams*. Addison-Wesley.

Beizer, B. 1995. *Black-Box Testing: Techniques for Functional Testing of Software and Systems*. Wiley.

Meszaros, G. 2007. *xUnit Test Patterns: Refactoring Test Code*. Addison-Wesley.

Marques, A. 2021. *Selenium WebDriver Quick Start Guide: Test Automation with Selenium Using Java*. Packt Publishing.

Jain, R., and Mathur, P. 2022. *API Testing and Development with Postman: A Practical Guide for Testers and Developers*. BPB Publications.

Whitaker, J. A. 2009. *How to Break Software: A Practical Guide to Testing*. Addison-Wesley.

Spillner, A., Linz, T., and Schaefer, H. 2021. *Software Testing Foundations: A Study Guide for the Certified Tester Exam*. Rocky Nook.

Humble, J., and Farley, D. 2010. *Continuous Delivery: Reliable Software Releases through Build, Test, and Deployment Automation*. Addison-Wesley.

Garg, S. 2020. *Hands-On Test Management with Jira: Implement Agile Test Management and Test Automation Strategies Effectively*. Packt Publishing.

Fewster, M., and Black, R. 2011. *Advanced Software Testing—Vol. 2: Guide* *to the ISTQB Advanced Certification as an Advanced Test Manager*. Rocky Nook.

Bach, J., and Kaner, C. 2013. *Lessons Learned in Software Testing: A Context-Driven Approach*. Wiley.

Arbon, P. 2016. *Agile Testing: How to Succeed in an eXtreme Testing Environment*. Addison-Wesley.

Grechanik, M. 2020. *Software Testing: Principles and Practices*. Springer.

Bach, J. 2016. *Exploratory Testing Explained: A Guide for Testers and QA Engineers*. StarTester Publications.

Raj, S. P. 2021. *Performance Testing with JMeter 5: Test Web and Mobile Applications for Scalability and Reliability*. Packt Publishing.

Deshpande, P. 2020. *Mastering Mobile Test Automation: Automate Android and iOS Mobile Apps with Appium*. BPB Publications.

Rex, B., and Spillner, A. 2014. *Software Testing Foundations: A Study Guide for the Certified Tester Exam (ISTQB Foundation Level)*. Rocky Nook.

Quality Assurance Testing from Beginner to Paid Professional, Part 1:
Everything You Need to Know to Start a Career in Manual and Automated QA Testing

ISBN: 979-8-3492-2790-5

Published in the United States

www.ingramcontent.com/pod-product-compliance
Lightning Source LLC
LaVergne TN
LVHW060042210926
848481LV00013B/3929
* 9 7 9 8 3 4 9 2 2 7 9 0 5 *